PEANUTS®
QUILTED CELEBRATIONS

KATHLEEN SHEA

Foreword by Jean Schulz

American Quilter's Society
www.AmericanQuilter.com

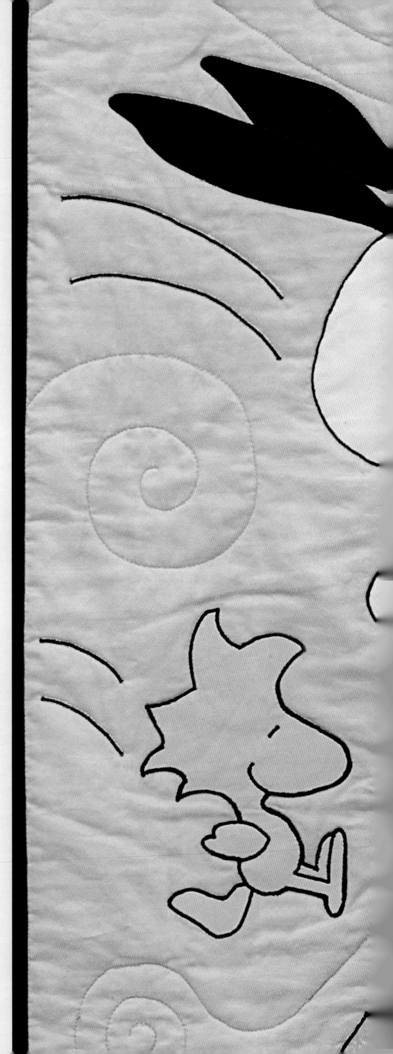

Located in Paducah, Kentucky, the American Quilter's Society (AQS) is dedicated to promoting the accomplishments of today's quilters. Through its publications and events, AQS strives to honor today's quiltmakers and their work and to inspire future creativity and innovation in quiltmaking.

EXECUTIVE BOOK EDITOR: ELAINE H. BRELSFORD
SENIOR EDITOR: LINDA BAXTER LASCO
COPY EDITOR: CHRYSTAL ABHALTER
GRAPHIC DESIGN: ELAINE WILSON
COVER DESIGN: MICHAEL BUCKINGHAM
PHOTOGRAPHY: CHARLES R. LYNCH, UNLESS OTHERWISE NOTED

Additional copies of this book may be ordered from the American Quilter's Society, PO Box 3290, Paducah, KY 42002-3290, or online at www.AmericanQuilter.com.

Text and quilt designs © 2015, Author, Kathleen Shea
Peanuts Characters © 2015, Peanuts Worldwide
Layout Artwork © 2015, American Quilter's Society

Library of Congress Cataloging–in–Publication Data

Shea, Kathleen, 1960-

Peanuts : quilted celebrations / by Kathleen Shea.

pages cm

Includes bibliographical references and index.

ISBN 978-1-60460-181-7 (alk. paper)

1. Quilts. 2. Appliqué--Patterns. 3. Cartoon characters in art. I. Title.

TT835.S4636 2015

746.46--dc23

2015001372

DEDICATION

First, to my mom, who has shared so much with me, and who, so many years ago and with the patience of a saint (much more than I will *ever* have), taught her little girl to sew.

Next, for my two greatest and most remarkable creations, Brian and Conor—it has been a delight watching you grow and learn so much about the world *and* watching you grow to understand and appreciate the amazement of Peanuts! You will be better prepared for life if you "Speak softly and carry a beagle!!"

Finally, for Tom. Thank you for your *endless* patience and *undying* support of me, and what I know is all my "baggage"—quirks, habits, collections, and obsessions. You bear it all so well, and I know the last 30-plus years have been quite an adventure!

I love you all.

ACKNOWLEDGMENTS

First and foremost, my sincere thanks to Jean Schulz. Without her support and encouragement, this book would *never* have come to be.

Also, my gratitude to Andrea Podley, the founder of the Peanuts Collector Club, who has probably thought more than once that I might be crazy, but who has been there to answer every question I have ever had, nonetheless.

Next, for her patience and endless willingness to assist me with artwork and drawings, and redrawings (and redrawings and redrawings!!), my heartfelt appreciation to Pam Drucker of Creative Associates. Creative Associates is a wonderful place, and Pam and the rest of the staff there have made me feel welcome whenever I have had occasion to visit.

Lastly, to the rest of my Peanuts friends and fellow members of the Peanuts Collector Club, truly, you are the most wonderful group of people in the world! Happiness is having friends like all of you!

CONTENTS

FOREWORD by Jean Schulz

Regular readers who followed *Peanuts*, the comic strip written by my husband, Charles M. (Sparky) Schulz, will no doubt recall one of the "classic" images of Charlie Brown—usually fully awake, bundled up in his bed, often pondering the uncertainties of life and, time and again, lying underneath a big, comfy-looking quilt.

In today's very busy, technologically oriented world, quilts remind us of simpler days, and offer warmth, coziness, and, dare I say, *security*. An embodiment of American ingenuity, quilting was originally seen as a way to conserve precious cloth by cutting up what was old and reusing it to create something new—perfect recycling, and dear to my heart. Nowadays, modern quilts are often made of brand-new fabric, purchased specifically for the task. A quilt often takes countless hours of painstaking, detailed work to complete, and today quilting has truly grown into an art form.

This is why I am excited that quilting and appliqué (a type of quilting in which shapes cut from one fabric are sewn onto another piece of fabric) are now, officially, part of the world of Peanuts! It was soon after Sparky passed away in 2000 that Kathleen Shea first contacted me about creating a book of patterns for quilts that would portray the *Peanuts* characters. Her concept for the book was not to "reinterpret" *Peanuts*, but rather to present the gang exactly as they had been drawn, created from fabric instead of paper and ink. She had already made a quilted pillow showing Snoopy typing away as he sat atop his doghouse, and, as she explained to me, it was obvious how perfectly the *Peanuts* comics could be adapted into quilts and quilting: "It's as if the cartoons had been drawn with the idea of fabric appliqué in mind."

Now, having seen the finished results of eleven holiday-themed projects that Kathleen created for the book, I can say that I am so glad she pursued her idea! This book of quilts, wallhangings, placemats, pillows, and more, presents the Peanuts gang in fabric and thread, and, like Sparky's drawings, Kathleen's designs are simple, yet they manage to convey so many happy emotions. Charlie Brown, Snoopy, Linus, and Lucy now come to us in this fresh and cuddly new medium.

INTRODUCTION:
Why Peanuts Quilts?

When I was growing up in . . . well, let's just say the 1960s, I had some good friends. And I had one very best friend—a friend who was with me almost all the time, listened to each one of my problems, and never had a critical word to say. His name was Snoopy. He was about 9" tall, made of hard, white plastic, and wore a brown aviator helmet, goggles, and a blue, silky scarf. For several years, I carried him literally everywhere. I also read about him—in the dozens of books written by his creator, Charles M. Schulz, and in the comic strip in our daily newspaper—and collected all manner of Peanuts-related goodies that were being produced at the time.

I still have my little Snoopy (and most of the other goodies), but I must admit, as I grew older and left childhood behind, Snoopy and the rest of the Peanuts gang became a bit less important in my life. I still read the comic strip when I stumbled upon it, and still marveled at how Charles Schulz seemed to have his finger on the pulse of life for everyone in the entire world. But I guess I had kind of "moved-on." I had finished my education, was well into my career, and just didn't have time for pleasant, fun diversions like Peanuts.

Eventually, I had a family of my own and life went on. But when it was reported in 1999 that Charles Schulz had become seriously ill with cancer, I started to pay attention again. Irrationally, I assumed—no, actually truly, truly believed—that he would recover and be fine. I could not imagine the world without him, without Snoopy and his friends.

As the weeks went on, I started to think long and hard about Peanuts and how much it had been a part of my life—about the hours and hours of happiness it had brought me. And I also started to consider how one-sided that happiness had been. Why hadn't I ever taken the time to just write a letter to Mr. Schulz, expressing my thanks? How hard would that have been?

I thought I still had time to do something to show my thanks, but, really, a letter would not do. I have been sewing and quilting since I was about eight years old. Why not create something based on the Peanuts characters? I finally decided on an appliquéd pillow portraying Snoopy on top of his doghouse, typing at his typewriter. I found the exact Peanuts image I was looking for, enlarged it, and started making a pattern. While selecting fabrics, I also made time to visit the local library to research Charles Schulz's address.

Unfortunately (not just for me, but really for the whole world), Mr. Schulz passed away before I had the pillow completed. He died on February 12, 2000, the very night before his last strip was published. I remember quite vividly watching the news the next morning—stunned and feeling an enormous sense of loss for this man that I had never met but who had given me so much.

I put the half-finished pillow aside for a while. I felt like crying every time I looked at it. But after a month or so, I took it out again. I knew Charles Schulz had been married. I would finish the pillow and send it to his wife. I did a bit more research at the library. Her name was Jean.

The pillow took me another few weeks to finish. I packed it up and wrote Jean Schulz a long, heartfelt letter, expressing the appreciation I had for what her late husband had done, attempting to convey some of the depth of my feelings. I assumed she must be an incredibly busy person. I did not expect a reply. I also assumed that my pillow would probably be one of hundreds or thousands of sympathy gifts she received, and she certainly could not be expected to acknowledge each one. I simply wanted to say thank you.

So when a nice beige envelope arrived in my mailbox a few weeks later with a return address of One Snoopy Place, I was stunned. Inside was a letter from Jean Schulz, expressing her thanks for my thoughtfulness. "Amazing," I thought. "What a wonderful person she must be to take the time to write to me." I carefully folded her letter away. It would be a special addition to my collection of Peanuts items.

Then I started to think about how incredibly easy it had been to adapt a Peanuts cartoon into a quilted piece. The characters were drawn simply, the strips were neat and uncluttered, there was minimal use of pattern and perspective—it was almost as if the characters had been created for the very purpose of appearing in quilts! In fact, I was stunned that no one else had thought of it!

And so, *Peanuts Quilted Celebrations* started to become a reality. Jean Schulz, in fact, thought that portraying the characters in a new medium— fabric—was a great idea. Yes, I wrote to her again. She has been tremendously supportive! She put me in touch with others who were be able to help me get my idea off the ground—Andrea Podley, president and founder of the Peanuts Collector Club, and numerous Peanuts friends—people who share my obsession for all things Peanuts and who are, truly, just about the nicest people in the world.

Please do not consider any of the designs or projects in this book to be my interpretation of Charles Schulz's work. My aim was not to redraw, redesign, or reinterpret, in any manner, the wonderful legacy left to us by Mr. Schulz, as if anyone could ever hope to improve upon the art he created! Rather, my goal from the very first has simply been to present the Peanuts characters exactly as originally drawn, in a new medium— fabric and thread!

My thanks to Charles M. Schulz for a lifetime of happy memories.

CHAPTER 1:
Fundamentals

SEWING EQUIPMENT

Sewing Machine

Adjustable tension, adjustable stitch width and length, needle stop down, a knee lifter, and adjustable needle positions are sewing machine features useful for satin-stitch appliqué and machine quilting. In addition, you'll need a straight-stitch presser foot, an open-toe appliqué foot, a walking foot, and European size 90/U.S. size 14 embroidery needles.

Light Box

Light boxes are available at craft and art supply stores. A less expensive alternative is to use a piece of glass (frosted glass produces less glare) placed over an opening that allows a light from below to come through.

Iron

As all of these quilts call for fusing, a good quality iron that heats evenly, produces enough steam, and has a wide variety of temperature controls is needed. A "mini iron" will come in handy for small areas. You also want a tube of iron cleaner to clean up the inevitable messiness that comes with using fusibles.

FABRIC SELECTION AND SEWING SUPPLIES

I truly hope your local newspaper is still publishing Peanuts. If so, please take a moment to look at the strip, and I mean *really* notice how simply the characters are drawn. Other than placing some elements behind others, there is minimal use of perspective; if any shading appears it is very subtle, and, with the exception of an occasional striped tee shirt and the ever-present zigzag across Charlie Brown's outfit, there is almost no use of pattern. The drawings have an almost chunky quality.

If there are clouds in the drawing, they probably look like pieces of popcorn. Also study the shrubs and trees. There are very few true points, but instead a lot of squared-off and boxy edges, and ink lines that simply end in a tiny blob.

So, what does Mr. Schulz's drawing style mean for us? It makes creating these quilts easier—both in fabric selection and embroidery techniques.

Fabric

Yardage calculations allow for shrinkage (for those who prewash their fabric). Most of the fabrics used in these projects are solid colors.

Why? Simply because *this represents the way the cartoons were drawn by Mr. Schulz.*

Sometimes the use of *textured* fabrics can make the project a bit more fun, and that's really what Peanuts is all about. Be guided by Charles Schulz's drawings. Your goal should be a cohesive, well-balanced use of color and subtle texture so the focal point is the presentation of the characters themselves.

Thread

With rare exceptions, usually in the background areas, all the satin stitching is done in black thread. Simply, the black helps to recreate the feeling of a cartoon by perfectly imitating the wonderful black ink lines drawn by Charles Schulz.

The key to thread selection is to use the same type of thread throughout your entire project.

When satin stitching, use black bobbin thread or lingerie thread in the bobbin, which is thinner than sewing thread and will help ensure that the bobbin stitches do not pull to the top of the satin stitching.

All projects in this book are machine quilted with monofilament thread. The bobbin is again filled with bobbin or lingerie thread.

Fusibles

Fusibles have almost revolutionized appliqué, allowing us to adhere one fabric to another with ease. But as with many innovations, there are some downsides to their use.

The fusibles used with these projects are paper-backed, which allow you to peel off one paper liner and adhere the fusible to the wrong side of the appliqué fabric. Then, a second paper liner is removed, and the appliqué piece is adhered to the background. Thus, there is no need for pinning or basting the piece in place.

For all projects in this book, I used Lite Steam-A-Seam 2® fusible web, which is available in both 9" x 12" sheets and by the yard. This fusible allows for repositioning of the appliqué piece until the final pressing is done, which can be a tremendous convenience. It has a light but even hold and will not bubble after washing.

Even with the convenience of paper-backed products, however, there are times when I simply prefer to not use them. For large appliqué pieces, I lightly seal the edges of the appliqué with a fabric or seam sealant. The appliqué is then adhered to the background using a fabric spray adhesive. For these quilts, I used 606® Spray and Fix adhesive (www.sprayandfix.com). As these sprays can be messy, I always apply the spray with my appliqué fabric lying face down on several sheets of newspaper. A fabric glue stick may also be used to hold down any stubborn edges of the appliqué when using this method.

Non-Stick Pressing Sheet

Non-stick pressing sheets are made of a heat-resistant material to which pre-fused appliqué pieces will stick when hot, but can be removed easily after cooling. These enable us to build the appliqué design, perfecting the placement of all the pieces before adhering them to the background fabric.

To use the pressing sheet in this manner, place it over the large cartoon drawing of the project. Position the appliqué pieces on the sheet, glue-side down, with the paper-backed fusible material already applied. Fuse all the pieces together with your iron according to the cartoon underneath, and allow it to cool. After cooling, carefully peel the now layered appliqué off the sheet, position it on the background fabric, and press with your iron to adhere it and make it permanent.

You can also use the lighter weight sheets as pressing cloths to protect delicate fabrics when fusing.

Stabilizers

Adhering a fusible to the wrong side of a fabric does NOT mean that the fabric is stabilized and ready for appliqué. *A stabilizer must still be used beneath for all satin-stitch appliqué.* If no stabilizer is used, the fabric will inevitably be drawn up on both sides of the appliqué stitch (otherwise known as "tunneling"), and the piece will be pulled out of shape.

I prefer to work with stabilizers that tear away easily when I have finished stitching.

Marking Tools

I find it easiest to use transfer paper and a simple mechanical pencil with a hard lead for transferring the details of the actual Peanuts figures, especially the markings for the faces,

I have had success with Saral® transfer paper (www.saralpaper.com). The papers are wax-free, so the lines are easy to remove, and are available in both rolls and sheets. I generally use the graphite color for a light, yet visible, line that is easy to stitch over and white to transfer marks to dark fabrics. Any stray marks will be so light that they can be removed with a white artist's eraser.

In addition to transfer paper, you'll need good quality tracing paper, which is available in pads or rolls.

Batting

I used a low-loft cotton batting for all of these projects, with an allowed quilting space of 6"–10". My batting of choice is Warm & Natural® Needled Cotton Batting (www.warmcompany.com). I usually purchase it in the larger, more economical sizes, and then cut it down to size as needed.

EXTRAS

In recent years, it seems that new products to make life easier become available on a daily basis, and it has been no different in the world of quilting. I now find these additional items to be indispensable:

Machine quilting gloves allow you to more easily grip and control the fabric.

The Supreme Slider (www.freemotionslider.com) is an anti-stick, flexible sheet that placed on the bed of your machine allows for easier movement of the quilt.

Quilters Hangup® Quilt Sleeves (www.quiltershangup.com) are premade, 4" wide, and great timesavers!

CHAPTER 2:
Fusing, Appliqué & Quilt Construction

FUSING OVERVIEW

For each quilt, you will find both individual patterns for the appliqué pieces and quilt drawings. The quilt drawings are line drawing representations of the quilts and are meant to be used with a Teflon® pressing sheet. The pressing sheet is placed over the quilt drawing, and the appliqués are layered on top, according to the quilt drawing.

Fuse the appliqué pieces to the backgrounds using one of two methods. Fuse small- and medium-sized appliqué pieces with Lite Steam-A-Seam 2. This particular fusible will not overly stiffen the fabric. Whenever any paper-backed fusible is used, the appliqué must be drawn in reverse. The patterns meant to be applied with a fusible are already reversed for you. DO NOT REVERSE THEM AGAIN WHEN TRACING OR REPRODUCING THEM.

For larger appliqué pieces, I've had more success using a spray fabric adhesive to attach them to the background. These larger pattern pieces are NOT reversed on the pattern sheet and SHOULD NOT be reversed. Both fusing methods are described in more detail below.

ADHERING APPLIQUÉS WITH FUSIBLE WEB

For Pieces Other Than Character Faces

Lite Steam-A-Seam 2 has two paper liners, one on each side of the fusible material. One liner peels off easily (referred to in the patterns as the "easy" liner), and the other does not (referred to in the patterns as the "not easy" liner). To use this product, first test the liners for removal at one of the corners first to determine which is which.

Trace the pattern shape onto the "not easy" liner. After tracing, remove the "easy" liner and adhere the Lite Steam-A-Seam 2 to the wrong side of the appliqué fabric, following the manufacturer's fusing instructions. Cut out the appliqué along the traced pattern lines. Peel off the "not easy" liner. If you have trouble removing the liner, score it with a pin, then start peeling it off at the perforation made by the pin.

Working on top of the quilt drawing, lay the appliqué piece onto the pressing sheet. Repeat the tracing and fusing steps with the other pieces to build the design, looking through the pressing sheet to the quilt drawing for correct placement. Press to fuse the whole appliqué when done. See the instructions that come with the Steam-A-Seam 2 for additional details.

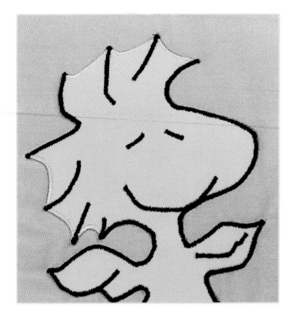

Fig. 1. Feather lines on Woodstock's head

Many of the pattern pieces have details that must be transferred to the fabric and satin stitched. Details of this type would include the lines that separate Snoopy's paw, or the feather lines on the top of Woodstock's head (Fig. 1). To transfer these details to the appliqué, first trace them onto tracing paper. Place the tracing paper over the appliqué shape, and slip a small piece of transfer paper between the tracing paper and the fabric. Trace over the detail lines with a hard pencil and remove the transfer paper.

Some of the larger detail pieces will need to be sewn on top of the appliqué piece (the black spot on Snoopy's back, for example). These details can also be fused and satin stitched before fusing the main piece to the background. The more detail work that can be completed before fusing the main appliqué piece to the background, the easier the stitching will be.

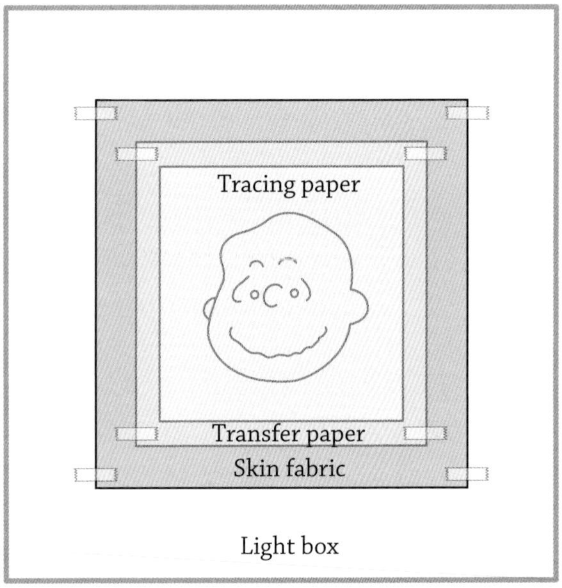

Character Faces

Accurately reproducing the facial features and expressions of the Peanuts characters is key to the success of these quilts. Charles Schulz was a genius, with the astonishing ability to completely change the appearance and mood of a character by making the slightest adjustment of an ink line. The expressions range from surprised and happy, to terribly sad and disappointed. Think about Charlie Brown's face when his baseball team loses every game!

And yet, while expressing so much, the facial expressions of the Peanuts characters are so simply drawn. The faces must be reproduced accurately, but proceeding carefully it's not

Fig. 2. Light box with skin fabric, transfer paper, and tracing paper with correctly placed image

difficult. The heads and faces are made and appliquéd separately, before stitching them to the background. Accordingly, if you're not satisfied with a finished face, simply cut another head piece and start again.

1. First, with simple tracing paper, trace the shape of the head. Also trace the facial details such as the mouth and eyes. Set aside.

2. Cut a piece of skin fabric slightly larger than what you will need for the head appliqué, by about 1" extra on each side. Using the light box, place this head fabric right-side up on the glass, holding the fabric in place with small pieces of clear tape at the edges.

3. Cover the piece of skin fabric with a slightly smaller piece of transfer paper, graphite-side down against the fabric. Again, attach the transfer paper with small pieces of tape. Finally, place the tracing you made of the head and face on top of the transfer paper so that the direction of the face is matching the photograph of the finished quilt. Tape down the tracing paper. See Fig. 2, page 14.

4. Using a dull pencil or ballpoint pen, carefully trace over the tracing, outlining the head and facial features, pressing firmly.

5. Remove the pieces of tape, tracing paper, and transfer paper. The traced head and face will appear lightly on your fabric.

Hints!
Shadowing and Doubling Skin Fabrics

If the skin fabric you have chosen is light in weight and/or color, darker fabrics placed underneath the finished piece may show through. This "shadowing" is to be avoided as it will affect the finished skin tone. To test your skin fabric, lay it over the edge of a darker fabric. If the dark fabric can be seen through the skin fabric, layering two pieces of skin fabric together will prevent the shadow.

Cut a second piece of skin fabric using the same face pattern. Lightly spray one side of the second piece of fabric with spray adhesive and adhere it to BACK of the skin fabric on which the face is drawn. Later, the head will be appliquéd to the background, and in order to appliqué the head properly, the very edges of the two pieces of skin fabric must be held firmly together. After cutting the head out, if the edges of the two layers are not completely adhered, DO NOT use additional spray adhesive to hold them together. It will be almost impossible to apply spray adhesive without over-spraying onto the top of the face. Instead, sparingly apply fabric glue stick, as needed, to keep the edges of the two pieces together.

It is far easier to stitch the face before fusing the head to the background. Simply stabilize the head fabric and carefully embroider the facial details. Refer to the instructions for machine embroidery (pages 17–19).

After the face is embroidered and you are happy with the results, cut a piece of the paper-backed fusible the size of the face fabric, remove the "easy" liner, and apply to the wrong side of the fabric. Cut out the head on the outline that was traced onto the skin fabric. The head will now

have the face already embroidered and is ready to be layered, fused, and satin stitched to the background using the pressing sheet.

ADHERING APPLIQUÉS WITH SPRAY ADHESIVE

For these quilts, I used 606 Spray and Fix, which is a permanent bonding adhesive. Carefully follow any instructions that come with the product. Using tracing paper, trace the pattern outlines and details. These patterns are NOT REVERSED and should NOT be reversed for use in the quilts. Pin the tracing on the RIGHT side of the appropriate fabric and cut out on the pattern outline.

If there are any details on the pattern piece that must be transferred to the fabric, such as the lines that separate Snoopy's paw and the feather lines on the top of Woodstock's head, slip a piece of transfer paper between the tracing paper and the fabric and trace over the lines with a firm pencil. Note that if there are any detail pieces that must be sewn on the top of the appliqué (such as the small roses on the Easter Beagle pillow in Fig. 3) these details can be fused and satin stitched before fusing the main piece to the background.

Hints!
Use of Specialty Fabrics for Appliqués

Some of the fleece or novelty fabrics that you select may not be suitable for the pressing required in the use of fusible web. If this is the case, you may certainly use a fabric glue stick or spray adhesive to adhere any such appliqués to the background. However, always keep in mind that ALL OF THE SMALLER APPLIQUÉ PATTERN PIECES HAVE ALREADY BEEN REVERSED FOR USE WITH FUSIBLE WEB. Therefore, if you wish to apply one of these smaller pieces with a glue or spray adhesive instead of fusible web, you must first reverse the pattern before cutting it from the fabric. Then cut the pattern out from the right side of the fabric and adhere it using spray adhesive or fabric glue.

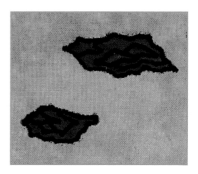

Fig. 3. Roses on the EASTER BEAGLE pillow

Before fusing any of these appliqués to the background, lightly apply seam sealant to the edges. Allow to dry and apply the spray adhesive over the back of the piece. Place the appliqué onto the background and press firmly, using the cartoon of the finished quilt as a guide for placement. Use a fabric glue stick as needed at the edges to keep the appliqué firmly in place.

LAYERING YOUR DESIGN

Since Teflon pressing sheets arrived on the scene, correctly placing intricate appliqué designs on the background has become appreciably easier. When layering the design, the pressing sheet is placed over the quilt drawing for that quilt. The sheet is transparent, so the quilt drawing is easily visible, making it almost impossible to position a piece incorrectly. Place the appliqué pieces directly on top of the sheet. After they are properly layered, adhere them to each other while still on the sheet. Cool the entire, fully-layered appliqué and peel it off the pressing sheet, ready to be adhered to the background as a single unit.

Note that if the placement of one of the upper layers of the appliqué unit is blocked from view (for example, the ornaments on the Christmas tree in MERRY CHRISTMAS, page 84), it will not be possible to view the exact placement using the quilt drawing, as the drawing will be blocked by the fabric. Simply make a tracing of the quilt drawing (on the CD) before you begin to layer the design. You can then use the tracing from above as you are building the design to check for correct placement.

MACHINE EMBROIDERY

After you have fused your completed appliqué to the background, satin stitching is the next step. Almost all satin stitching for these projects is done with black thread (there are some exceptions that will be noted in the specific project instructions). You will be happier with your sewing experience and final results if you use a good quality thread. Either satin or matte thread may be used, but be consistent throughout the project. Use a lightweight bobbin or lingerie thread in the bobbin.

The satin stitch produces the best results when the upper-thread tension is loosened slightly. As for stitch width, my machine is generally set between 1.5 – 2.5. This number may vary slightly from quilt to quilt, and in certain areas. For example, I often use a slightly wider stitch for the pieces in the foreground, and a slightly narrower stitch for facial details.

If you have not done a lot of intricate satin stitching, *please* take the time to make a few practice pieces. This can be as simple as fusing a circle, square, and triangle to a background piece and satin stitching around each one to familiarize yourself with the process of correctly stitching inner and outer corners and curves. The following guidelines might be helpful.

1. Your stitch length should be such so that the satin stitch is smooth, not bunched up. Most machines have a suggested stitch length just for satin stitching. The stitch should be placed so that the INNER edge of the stitch is covering the edge of the appliqué piece, and the OUTER edge is just falling off the appliqué to catch the background.

2. Stabilizer *should always* be used. Any fusible paper that might still be on the back of the appliqué pieces does *not* count as a stabilizer! A stabilizer should always be placed underneath, between the project and the sewing machine, before satin stitching the appliqué in place. The general rule is that the more layers of fabric you have on top, the less stabilizer you need underneath; conversely the less fabric on top, the heavier the stabilizer underneath. There are now so many stabilizers available that the choice of which to use can be overwhelming. Choose one that tears away easily. If additional stabilizing is needed, rather than using a heavier stabilizer, use two or three layers of a lighter weight product that will tear away without damaging the stitching.

3. Do the satin stitching after all your appliqué pieces are fused to the background. Before beginning, take a careful look at your overall appliqué and plan to stitch pieces that are in the *background* first. For example, on MERRY CHRISTMAS, Charlie Brown's clothing is behind Snoopy (Fig. 4). Therefore, his jacket and pants should be satin stitched before Snoopy is done.

Try to start stitching along a straight edge. When you begin, always pull the bobbin thread up to the top. Do not backstitch. Backstitching with a satin stitch tends to create an unattractive thread lump. Instead, take a few stitches in one place while at zero width, then widen the stitch as needed. Always try to work from the middle out toward the edges. This applies to individual appliqués as well as quilts as a whole.

4. When stitching outside corners, stitch toward the outer corner and just past it, stopping with the needle down in the background fabric (Fig. 5). Note the position of the dot at the outer corner, representing where the needle should be when you stop stitching. Leaving the needle in the fabric, raise the presser foot, and pivot the project as needed. Lower the presser foot and resume stitching. Your fabric should be aligned so that, as you continue, your satin stitch falls almost fully on the appliqué fabric, just catching the background fabric.

When stitching inside corners, stitch along the straight edge toward the corner, and stop stitching approximately ⅛" past the inner corner, with the needle down in the appliqué fabric (Fig. 6). Note the position of the dot indicating the position of the needle. Keeping the needle in the down position, raise the presser foot, and pivot the fabric as needed. Lower the presser foot, and resume stitching. The satin stitches should fall almost fully on the appliqué fabric, just catching the background fabric.

LEFT: **Fig. 4.** Charlie Brown's clothing is behind Snoopy in the MERRY CHRISTMAS wallhanging.

When stitching outside curves, as you round the curve, stop as needed with the needle in the background fabric on the outside edge of the curve, raising the presser foot, gradually pivoting the project, then lowering the presser foot to continue stitching, working through the curve (Fig. 7). Note the positions of the dots, indicating the positions of the needle-stopping positions. The satin stitches should fall almost fully on the appliqué fabric, just catching the background fabric.

When stitching inside curves, as you round the curve, stop as needed with the needle in the appliqué fabric on the inside edge of the curve, raising the presser foot and gradually pivoting the project, then lowering the presser foot as you continue to stitch, working through the curve (Fig. 8). Note the positions of the dots, indicating positions of the needle-stopping positions. The satin stitches should fall almost fully on the appliqué fabric, just catching the background fabric.

When stitching small, sharp curves (such as those around a character's eye or nose), it may be necessary to stop as indicated with your needle down and reposition the piece quite often—even after just one or two stitches. Be patient and proceed slowly! Some of the embroidery in these pieces can be quite intricate. Do not rush!

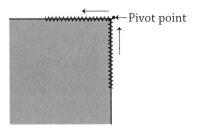

Fig. 5. Outside corner

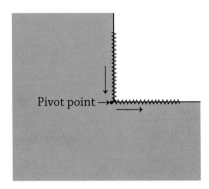

Fig. 6. Inside corner

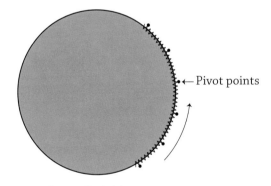

Fig. 7. Outside curve

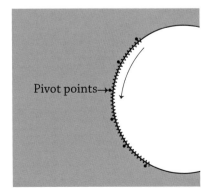

Fig. 8. Inside curve

EMBELLISHING AND MAKING IT YOUR OWN

Many of the projects already have embellishment suggestions that can easily be adapted to allow for other decorations. Peanuts is synonymous with fun, and embellishing will definitely enhance your quilt's happiness quotient. Carefully consider the elements of each appliqué within your quilt and think about how you can turn them from flat into dimensional, texturized, and/or colorful elements that will make the overall piece sparkle!

Any embellishment should be part of your overall quilt design and execution. In these quilts, the emphasis is always on the Peanuts characters, but give some consideration to the elements around the characters. For example, in MERRY CHRISTMAS (page 84), several stars appear in the night sky.

While the stars are of silver metallic fabric, brainstorm other ways that they might have been made—glitter, sequins, or metallic confetti glued to the background might have been used; star-shaped buttons or charms would have been another option; even simple embroidery (either

by hand or machine) using a metallic thread would have added an understated emphasis. For the RED, WHITE, AND BLUE bed scarf (page 50), glittering fabric paint was used to make the fireworks, with tiny, glass seed beads set into the paint before it dried (Fig. 9). The bed scarf also features an actual American flag attached to a pole (which is really a candy stick).

As the focus of these quilts is on holiday themes, search for seasonal buttons, ribbons, fabrics, beads, charms, etc., that might enhance the seasonal theme of the projects. Look for both common and unusual items. Consider costume jewelry, miniatures, even fabric yo-yos, if appropriate. You probably already have a stash of quilting fabric; complement it with a collection of notions and paraphernalia to embellish your work, and have fun hunting them down.

Clearly, it is important to base any embellishment on the intended use of the individual project. If it's a wallhanging that won't be laundered, there's almost no limit on the type of detail, decoration, or freestanding element you can add. A bed quilt must be washed; and while embellishments are still possible, they must be able to survive both daily use and laundering.

Keep in mind the weight any embellishments will add to the piece. It may be necessary to include additional batting or fabric to the quilt to hold the weight of the embellishments, or to attach the decorations by stitching all the way through the quilt instead of just gluing or tacking to the front. However, don't consider the extra work involved with embellishing as a reason to leave your quilt plain and lacking in decoration. Adorning it will lead to a truly one-of-a-kind creation.

Fig. 9. Detail of fireworks from RED, WHITE, AND BLUE

EMBELLISHMENT SUGGESTIONS

Hanging, Three-Dimensional, and Padded Elements

Look at the possibilities within the quilt you are making. For example, if Snoopy appears, instead of satin stitching his ears, could they be tacked onto the background at the top so they hang free? Such an ear would need to be sewn with a facing, or it could be made from a piece of leather or vinyl. Another option is applying the appliqué piece with satin stitching, then laying another piece (cut from the same pattern) over it. For example, in HAPPINESS IS (page 26), the hearts are satin stitched to the background, then additional pop-up hearts are created and tacked down at the top and bottom edges (Fig. 10).

The clothing of the characters provides a wealth of opportunity for embellishment. Use real buttons or beads on their shirts; add a pom-pom or yarn tassel onto the top of a hat; or use thin cording or embroidery thread to represent the stripes of Linus's tee shirt.

If you are making a bed quilt and want to add some depth and dimension that will stand up to use, consider adding a thin piece of batting to elements in the foreground to make them stand out a bit. In the AUTUMN LEAF JUMP quilt (page 61), this technique could be used for Snoopy and Woodstock. This would involve using spray adhesive to adhere the already layered appliqués to a piece of batting, then carefully cutting away the batting just inside the outer edge of the appliqué. Adhere the piece to the background with spray adhesive and satin stitch it to the background.

Fig. 10. Heart from HAPPINESS IS

Consider adding freestanding, three-dimensional elements. To create small details, such as the tree lights and star on MERRY CHRISTMAS, use one or more layers of water-soluble sheets. Sandwich and pin the appliqué fabric piece between layers of water-soluble sheets, satin stitch the edges through the sheets, and wash the piece to remove the water-soluble material.

Use yo-yos to create any flowers that appear. With appropriate shaping, they can be transformed into a variety of floral shapes. Note the shamrocks in ST. PATRICK'S DAY (page 32).

For larger elements, such as a plant or flower in the foreground, trace or transfer its shape onto appropriate fabric. Create a sandwich with flannel or thin batting and another piece of the same fabric underneath. Satin stitch around your outline, apply seam sealant to the edges, then carefully cut out the entire piece just outside of the stitching line. Seal the edges again and tack to the background.

Specialty Fabrics, Prints, and Quilting

Certain fabrics can add depth and a tactile quality to your quilt. Of course, the end use of the quilt and how it will be cleaned must be considered. But a bit of pizzazz can be added to just about every project by replacing a solid-colored cotton fabric with something a bit more interesting.

All the clothes in MERRY CHRISTMAS (Fig. 11), are of textured, napped fabrics; the bulbs on the tree are of shiny, metallic fabrics; the tree is of corduroy; the snow is napped; the shadows are of netting. All combine to make the piece much more interesting than it would have been if simple, solid cottons had been used throughout. The fact that this piece will not be washed allows for the use of just about any fabric imaginable. However, even in bed quilts, fabrics with a little oomph can be used!

In AUTUMN LEAF JUMP, page 61, Snoopy is made of window darkening fabric. Not only does this prevent shadowing of other fabric under the white, but it also provides a subtle, napped surface for our favorite beagle. Also in this quilt, while the characters themselves are (as always) made of solid fabrics, there were a few liberties taken with the leaves. Some are of solid cotton, others are of subtle ombres and marbled batiks. These selections add depth and interest to not only the leaf pile, but also to both the Double Chain of Squares and striped borders.

The quilting is another opportunity to add a bit of embellishment. In both of the above-mentioned quilts, the background quilting was done in swirls to suggest wind and the movement of air. Look at the elements of the quilt and create accordingly!

BELOW: **Fig. 11.** Detail of MERRY CHRISTMAS wallhanging

QUILT CONSTRUCTION

A Word About Borders

There was a time, not so long ago, when any quilter worth her (or his) fabric stash would strive to create perfect borders and bindings with precisely mitered corners. To those of you who have never had to attempt mitering, in my opinion, you're better off for having avoided this usually difficult, sometimes impossible, almost always headache-inducing (at least in my personal experience) task.

Thank goodness we are now able to put those days behind us. Some time ago, many quilters decided they weren't going to take it anymore! A new, simpler, perfectly acceptable alternative swept the quilting world. Accordingly, unless otherwise indicated, all borders and bindings in this book are created by first applying them to the sides of the quilt, then applying them to the top and bottom. There is no mitering of corners anywhere!

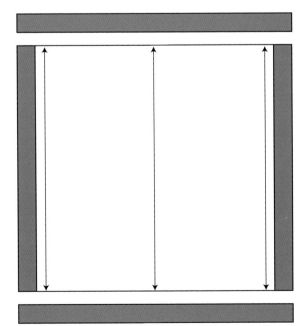

Fig. 12

While the miter-less method is infinitely easier, it also involves some effort to do correctly and ensure that your finished quilt lies flat. Before cutting and applying the borders, lay your quilt on a flat surface and, using a tape measure, measure each side edge of the quilt, and then up the middle (Fig. 12). Take these three measurements (for extra accuracy, take each measurement twice), average them, and cut your two side fabric border strips to this length. Pin the strips to the quilt first at the corners and middle (matching the middle of the strips to the middle of the edge of the quilt), and then along the entire edge. Sew the two border strips to the quilt.

Then, follow the same procedure to apply border strips to the top and bottom of the quilt. Measure across the quilt, average the measurements, cut the border strips to size, pin, and sew.

Basting and Quilting

When the appliqué, piecing, satin stitching, and embellishing are done, it's time to add the finishing touches to your masterpiece.

First, lay the piece face-down on a heavy Turkish towel. Use a white towel if you have one. If not, use one that has been washed repeatedly so that there will be no chance that the color of the towel will bleed onto your work. Press, using an up and down motion, TAKING GREAT CARE WITH EMBELLISHMENTS AND SPECIALTY FABRICS. After pressing, create a quilt sandwich by placing the backing fabric on a flat surface (wrong-side up), batting on top of the backing, and finally the finished quilt top (right-side up).

There are several tried-and-true methods of basting. I have always found quilter's safety pins to be the quickest and easiest, but use whichever method you're most comfortable with. If you do opt for pins, take caution not to leave them in too long. The holes can become permanent.

All quilting for these projects was done by machine with clear thread on top and bobbin/lingerie thread in the bobbin. I almost always quilt with a quilting foot and the feed dogs down (disengaged). Start with areas in the center of the quilt, and work your way toward the outer edges. Generally, I stitch around all characters and other main design areas of appliqué. I also quilt along one edge of the facial detail lines of satin stitching. This helps to create some dimension. In the backgrounds, when additional quilting is needed, I stitch around elements like stars and clouds. I love to make wind lines! Somehow, it just seems so relaxing to make big, lazy curves and whirls. Trace these out with a removable marker before stitching.

When the inner area is done, I generally do some quilting in the border areas as needed and to add dimension. Here, on the longer, straight runs, you may prefer to raise/engage the feed dogs. Some quilters also use a walking foot to keep the layers from sliding. Whichever method you use, start the border quilting in the center of the border and stitch out to the corner or end. Then, go back to the center, and stitch out to the opposite end.

When the quilting is finished, carefully trim away the excess batting and backing from all sides and square-up the quilt as needed.

Bindings

All bindings used for these quilts are double-fold and cut on the straight-of-grain (with the exception of the MERRY CHRISTMAS wallhanging).

Following the same measuring and cutting instructions given for adding borders, apply the binding first to the longer sides of the quilt. Pin the binding along one straight edge on the top side of the quilt, aligning all the raw edges. Sew with a slightly lengthened machine stitch.

For the shorter sides, cut each strip of binding 2" longer than needed. This will allow you to turn under 1" at each end of the strip to keep the raw edges hidden (Fig. 13). Pin and sew as with the longer sides, turning under 1" at each end.

Fold the binding over to the back, pin in place, and hand sew to the back of the quilt. Be sure the binding is covering the machine-stitching line. Finish with small, inconspicuous hand stitches in the same color as the binding.

Fig. 13. Detail of HAPPINESS Is binding

CHAPTER 3:
Putting It All Together

PROJECT LINUS, 40" x 40", made by the author

HAPPINESS IS—Wallhanging, 12" x 22½", made by the author
Full-size patterns on the CD

PEANUTS QUILTED CELEBRATIONS ❤ KATHLEEN SHEA

Happiness Is—Wallhanging

FABRIC AND SUPPLIES

Yardage

Note: All the prints used should be small scale.

- ¾ yard medium purple print for the borders, binding, and backing
- ¼ yard light pink print for folded borders and half-square triangles
- ¼ yard light yellow print for folded borders and half-square triangles
- ¼ yard light blue solid for sky and lettering area
- 16" x 26½" batting

Scraps

- Dark magenta solid for hearts
- Medium rose, solid or marbled, for hearts
- Pink for Lucy's skin
- Medium purple solid for Lucy's dress
- Black for Lucy's hair, Snoopy's ear, and details
- White for Snoopy
- Medium green solid for grass

Additional Supplies

- Teflon pressing sheet
- 1 – 9" x 12" sheet of Lite Steam-A-Seam 2
- 1 – 9" x 12" sheet of tracing paper
- 1 – 6" x 12" piece of transfer paper
- 4 – 8" x 8" pieces of wash-away stabilizer
- 6 – 9" x 12" sheets of tear-away stabilizer
- Fine-line permanent marker (optional)

Cutting and Assembly

All cutting for the appliquéd area is done using the pattern pieces, which are already reversed. Follow the instructions in chapter 2. Assemble the appliqués for Lucy and Snoopy. The eyes for both Snoopy and Lucy are satin stitched.

1. Cut a 9" x 10" (l x w) piece of light blue for the sky. Trace the pattern pieces for the grass, all hearts, Lucy, and Snoopy on the "not easy" liner of the fusible web. Remove the "easy" liner and adhere to the wrong side of the appropriate fabrics. Cut out pieces and transfer the details. Using the pressing sheet, layer the grass on top of the bottom portion of the sky. Press and allow to cool.

2. Create the head for Lucy. Double the skin fabric if shadowing occurs (page 15).

3. Layer all of the pattern pieces for Lucy, Snoopy, and the background on the pressing sheet. Press all pieces to fuse and allow to cool. Carefully remove from the pressing sheet and, using the quilt drawing (on the CD) as a guide, layer the pieces on the background. Press and allow to cool.

4. Working from the middle outward, satin stitch the characters and detail lines. Satin stitch the hearts in the background.

5. Square-up and trim the piece to measure 8½" x 9½" (l x w). Set aside.

6. Cut 2 strips 3" x 10" of light blue. Transfer the HAPPINESS IS and A WARM PUPPY lettering onto the strips of fabric. Satin stitch over the lettering, stabilizing as needed. Trim the lettering strips to measure 2" x 9½", keeping the lettering centered (Fig. 1).

7. Cut 4 strips 2" x 9½" of the purple print. Sew 2 of the strips to the upper and lower edge of the appliquéd section. Sew the light blue pieces with the completed satin-stitched lettering to the top and bottom of the piece, as shown. Sew the remaining 2 purple strips to the top and bottom edges of the lettering strips (Fig. 2).

Fig. 1

8. Cut 4 squares each of the yellow and pink print fabrics 3⅛" x 3⅛" (8 total).

    a. Place one square of each fabric right sides together. Press, keeping the squares aligned.

    b. With a rotary cutter, slice the squares in half diagonally (Fig. 3).

    c. Pin each pair of triangles together and stitch slowly on the cut edge, taking care not to stretch the bias edge.

    d. Again, taking care not to stretch, press the 8 half-square triangles (HSTs) open with the seam allowances toward the darker fabric. Trim the "dog ears." Square-up to measure 2¼" x 2¼".

9. Using matching thread, satin stitch the magenta hearts to the centers of the HSTs, making sure to alternate the orientation of the pink and yellow print fabrics as shown in figure 2. Again referring to figure 2, sew the heart units into 2 horizontal rows, placing the larger hearts at the ends. Square up to measure 2¼" x 9½".

10. For the final border, the double-fold pink and yellow prints lie on top of the purple print. Apply as follows (Fig. 4, page 30):

    a. Cut 3 strips 2" x width of fabric (WOF) of the purple print. Apply to the sides, then the top and bottom edges of the wallhanging.

    b. Cut 3 strips 1½" x WOF of the yellow print and 3 strips 1" x WOF of the pink print.

Fig. 2. Quilt assembly

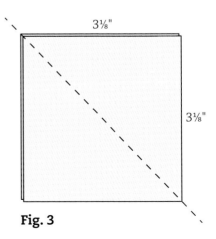

Fig. 3

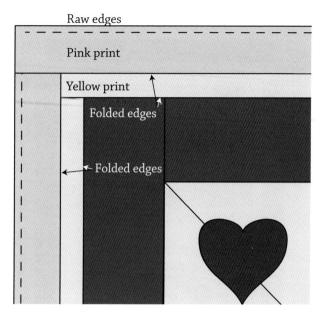

Raw edges

Pink print

Yellow print

Folded edges

Folded edges

Fig. 4

Fig. 5

c. Fold the strips in half lengthwise, wrong sides together, and press.

d. Cut 2 pink and 2 yellow strips equal to the long side measurement of the wallhanging.

e. With raw edges together, layer the pink folded strip on top of the yellow strip and align both with the raw edge of the purple border.

f. Stitch the double-fold strips to the purple using a ⅛" seam, keeping all raw edges together, and leaving 2" free of stitching at both ends of each set of strips. (This will allow you to weave the ends at the corners.)

g. Cut and sew the pink and yellow strips to the top and bottom edges of the wallhanging in the same manner, again leaving 2" of the ends free.

h. Weave the loose ends at each corner together as shown (Fig. 5). Pin and stitch all corners through all layers of fabric.

11. Press the wallhanging carefully from the wrong side.

FINISHING

1. Cut a piece 16" x 26½" from the medium purple print for the backing. Layer the quilt top with batting and backing. Baste the layers together as needed.

2. Quilt around Lucy and Snoopy, the grass, and the hearts in the appliquéd area. Quilt just inside all the purple print borders.

3. Add pop-up elements to the 4 magenta hearts in the corners, all of the hearts in the appliquéd area, and Snoopy's ear. Each is identical in size and color to the appliquéd piece underneath and is tacked on to the wallhanging to add dimension.

   a. For each element, cut 2 pieces of the fabric that matches the appliqué approximately ½" larger all around than the original pattern piece. Adhere the fabric pieces, wrong sides together, using fabric adhesive spray. Using the original appliqué pattern, trace and cut out the pop-up.

   b. Layer the pop-up between 4 layers of wash-away stabilizer (cut the stabilizer to about ½" larger all around; use 2 layers on top and 2 on the bottom). Using the pressing sheet, iron the stabilizer/fabric sandwich for a few seconds.

   c. Satin stitch around the edges of the pop-up with matching thread for the hearts in the corners and black thread for all the pop-ups in the appliquéd area.

   d. Free-motion machine embroider "Happy Valentine's Day!" on the large heart for the appliquéd area before tacking it to the background. As an alternative, draw the lettering with a fine-line fabric marking pen, or embroider by hand.

   e. Dissolve the stabilizer on the pop-ups by soaking them in water for a few minutes. Let dry and press lightly. Tack all the hearts in place at the point at the bottom of the heart and the inner corner at the top of the heart. Bend the hearts up at the center and finger press.

   f. For Snoopy's ear, tack the top corner edge of the pop-up to his appliquéd ear (Fig. 6).

4. Trim the batting and backing even with the quilt top. Cut 2 strips 2¼" x WOF for the binding and apply to the quilt (page 24).

5. For hanging loops, cut 2 strips 1½" x 6½" from the purple print. Fold each in half lengthwise, right sides together. Stitch along the long edge, turn, and press. Stitch to the back side along the top edge, hiding stitches in the binding seam.

Fig. 6

St. Patrick's Day—Pillow

21" x 21", made by the author

Full-size patterns on the CD

ST. PATRICK'S DAY
Pillow

PILLOW FABRICS AND SUPPLIES

Yardage
- 1 yard dark green solid for the pillow backing, borders, and shamrocks
- ½ yard light green print for the center square of the pillow (turned on point)
- ¼ yard opaque white solid for Snoopy
- 1 yard dark green/yellow print for the triangles and prairie points
- ⅛ yard marbled yellow for the borders and hatband
- ¾ yard muslin for the quilt top foundation
- 24" x 24" batting

Scraps
- Bright green for the hat
- Black for the ears/details

Additional Supplies
- 20" x 20" pillow form
- Teflon pressing sheet
- 2 – 9" x 12"" sheets of Lite Steam-A-Seam 2
- 1 – 9" x 12" sheet of tracing paper
- 1 – 6" x 12" piece of transfer paper
- 2 – 9" x 12" sheets of tear-away stabilizer
- green embroidery floss

PILLOW CUTTING AND ASSEMBLY

All cutting for the appliquéd area is done using the pattern pieces on the CD and following the instructions in chapter 2. Assemble the appliqués first. All patterns for appliqué pieces are already reversed. Snoopy's eyes are created of black fabric.

Snoopy and Shamrock

1. Trace all the pattern pieces for Snoopy, his hat and shamrocks, and the large background shamrock on the "not-easy" liner of the fusible web. Remove the "easy" liner, and adhere each piece of fusible web to the wrong side of the appropriate fabric. Cut out the appliqué pieces and transfer the detail lines.

2. Using the pressing sheet, layer all pieces for Snoopy, his hat, and the background shamrock. Note that the top and front of the hat lie on top of Snoopy's head, but the back brim of the hat curves underneath the back edge of his ear. Accordingly, as indicated on the hat pattern, cut a small slit along the bottom edge of the hat so that the back of the brim can tuck behind Snoopy's ear. Carefully press all pieces and allow to cool.

3. Cut a 12" x 12" background square of light green fabric. (This is actually ½" larger than needed, but the fabric may shrink or pull in slightly during appliqué.) Turn the square on-point, and center Snoopy and his hat, with his head toward one corner and feet toward the opposite corner.

Fuse in place. Complete the satin stitching. Satin stitch the large shamrock with matching green thread. Trim the appliquéd square to 11½" x 11½", keeping Snoopy centered.

4. Cut 2 yellow strips ¾" x the width of fabric (WOF). Apply as a border to 2 opposite sides of the appliquéd square; then apply to the 2 remaining sides. Press the entire square carefully from the wrong side.

5. From the dark green/yellow print, cut 2 squares 9½" x 9½". Cut the squares once on the diagonal to make 4 triangles. Find the center point of the bias-cut side on each triangle and the center point on the sides of the appliquéd square. Match up these center points, pinning 2 of the triangles to opposite sides of the square, right sides together. Take care not to stretch the bias side of the triangles. Stitch the triangles right sides together. Press each triangle to the outside. Apply the remaining 2 triangles in the same manner to the remaining corners.

6. For the first border, crosscut 2 yellow strips ¾" x WOF. Apply them to the sides of the square, then to the top and bottom (page 23).

7. For the second border, crosscut 2 solid dark green strips 2¼" x WOF. Apply to each side, then to the top and bottom.

8. Layer the pillow top square with the batting and a 25" x 25" square of muslin, and baste as needed. Quilt around the Snoopy, the background shamrock, and the borders.

9. Carefully trim the batting and muslin even with the pillow top.

10. Make 7 mini-shamrocks to scatter over the light green as follows:

Fig. 1

  a. Using a light-colored marker, draw 7 – 1½" circles on the wrong side of the dark green solid fabric. Place a second piece of the green fabric underneath, right sides together. Pin the 2 fabrics together.

  b. Using a shortened stitch length, stitch around the drawn circles. Cut out each circle ⅛" outside of the stitching.

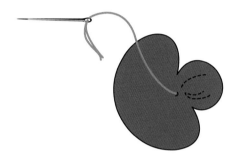

Fig. 2

  c. Pull the 2 pieces of fabric slightly apart and clip an opening in the center of the fabric on one side of each circle. Enlarge the clip to approximately ¾". Coat the clip lightly with seam sealant.

  d. Carefully turn right-side out, shaping as needed.

Fig. 3

  e. Thread a hand-stitching needle with a double strand of matching green thread; knot at the end. Bring the needle up through the center of the circle at the clip, exiting through the solid circle (Fig. 1).

  f. Imagine that each circle is divided into 3 even portions. Carry the thread over one of the "dividing lines" and bring the needle back up through the center (Fig. 2).

ST. PATRICK'S DAY pillow assembly diagram

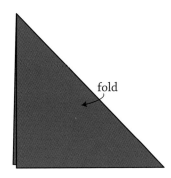

fold

fold

Fig. 4

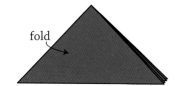

Raw edges

Baste

Right side of pillow top

Fig. 5

g. Pull the thread tightly. Continue with the other 2 imaginary "dividing lines," pulling thread tightly each time, and ending at the center. End off at the center of the shamrock (Fig. 3, page 35).

h. Using green thread and the photo as a guide, tack the 7 shamrocks to the pillow top, stitching a ¼" stem at the bottom of each.

11. The edge of the pillow is trimmed with prairie points. Use 8 prairie points for each side (total of 32). To make prairie points:

a. Cut 32 – 3½" squares of the dark green St. Patrick's Day print.

b. Fold diagonally, and then again into a triangle. Finger-press (Fig. 4).

c. Spacing the prairie points evenly, arrange 8 on each side of the pillow, with the "points" positioned toward the pillow (Fig. 5).

d. Pin in place. Baste in place, just inside the ¼" seam line.

12. Cut a dark green solid square 20½" x 20½". Pin to the appliquéd square, right sides together. Stitch around the pillow top, leaving approximately 12" open along one edge for turning and inserting the pillow form.

13. Clip the corners, turn, and press as needed. Insert the pillow form and hand stitch the opening closed.

St. Patrick's Day
Table Runner
17½" x 45", made by the author
Full-size patterns on the CD

St. Patrick's Day
Table Runner

TABLE RUNNER FABRICS AND SUPPLIES

Yardage

- 1½ yards dark green solid for the backing, outer border, and shamrocks
- ¼ yard light green print for the rectangles
- ¼ yard opaque white solid for Snoopy
- 1 yard dark green/yellow print for the border and prairie points
- ½ yard marbled yellow for the narrow borders and hatbands
- 21½" x 49" batting

Scraps

- Bright green for the hats
- Black for ears/details

Additional Supplies

- Teflon pressing sheet
- 4 – 9" x 12" sheets of Lite Steam-A-Seam 2
- 1 – 9" x 12" sheet of tracing paper
- 1 – 6" x 12" piece of transfer paper
- 4 – 9" x 12" sheets of tear-away stabilizer

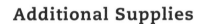

TABLE RUNNER CUTTING AND ASSEMBLY

Snoopy and Shamrocks

1. Trace all the pattern pieces for Snoopy and his hat on the "not easy" liner of the fusible web. Remove the "easy" liner, and adhere each piece of fusible web to the wrong side of the appropriate fabric. Cut out the appliqué pieces and transfer detail lines.

2. Using the pressing sheet, layer all pieces for Snoopy, his hat, and the background shamrock. Note that the top and front of the hat lie on top of Snoopy's head, but that the back brim of the hat curves underneath the back edge of his head. Accordingly, as indicated on the hat pattern, cut a small slit along the bottom edge of the hat so you can tuck the back of the brim behind Snoopy's ear. Carefully press all pieces and allow to cool.

3. Cut the 2 light green rectangles 10½" x 13½". Center the Snoopy/shamrock appliqués on the rectangles as shown and fuse in place.

4. Working from the middle outward, satin stitch the appliqués to the background. Satin stitch the shamrock with dark green thread. Trim the rectangles to measure 9" x 12". Set aside.

5. Cut a dark green/yellow print rectangle 4½" x 9¼". Crosscut 7 yellow strips ¾" x width of fabric (WOF). Use the strips to add a border (page 23), first to the ends, then to the long sides of the rectangle.

6. Crosscut a light green print strip 2½" x WOF. Add it as a border, first to the ends, then to the long sides of the yellow-bordered dark green print rectangle. Press. Trim to measure 9" x 13½".

7. Join the 3 rectangles with a ¾" yellow strip between them. Add a yellow border to the ends of the joined rectangles, then to the sides. See the runner assembly diagram (page 40).

8. Cut 3 dark green/yellow print fabric strips 2½" x WOF. Apply borders to the long sides of the rectangle, then to the narrow ends. Add another yellow border, using the strips already cut.

9. Cut 3 dark green solid strips 1¼" x WOF for the outer border. Apply to the sides, then the ends.

10. From the wrong side, press the quilt top carefully, taking care not to stretch it.

11. Make prairie points as before (page 36) from 48 – 3½" x 3½" squares of dark green/yellow St. Patrick's Day print.

12. Spacing the prairie points evenly, arrange 18 on each long side of the table runner and 6 on each short side, with the points positioned toward the middle of the table runner. Pin in place. Baste in place, just inside the ¼" seam line.

13. Cut a piece of dark green solid 21½" x 49" for the backing. Layer the quilt top with the batting and backing. Baste the layers together as needed.

Table runner assembly diagram

14. Quilt around both Snoopys, the large shamrocks, and the inner yellow borders. Do not quilt the outermost yellow border.

15. Carefully trim the batting *only* even with the quilt top, taking care *not* to trim the excess green backing. Fold and press the prairie points to the *outside* with the prairie point seam allowance pressed under and inward.

16. Turn the quilt top over, wrong-side up. Holding the solid green backing out of the way, carefully trim the batting again, approximately ¼" so that the batting is ¼" smaller than the backing around all the edges. Loosely pin the edges of the backing and the quilt top together, and now quilt around the inside edge of the outermost yellow border. Remove the pins.

17. Trim the solid green backing so that the raw edge extends approximately ½" beyond the quilt top size. Fold the raw edge of the solid green fabric toward the inside, carefully covering the edge of the batting. Carefully pin the edge of the backing to the edge of the quilt top, enclosing the batting. Hand sew in place.

18. Like the pillow, the table runner is embellished with mini-shamrocks. Make 15 mini-shamrocks as before (page 35). Scatter the shamrocks over the table runner, as shown in the photograph (page 37). With 2 strands of dark green thread, tack the center of the shamrocks to the runner, and, with the same thread, use a backstitch to create a ¼" stem for each.

EASTER BEAGLE & FRIEND—Pillow Set
SNOOPY PILLOW
24" x 24", made by the author
Full-size patterns on the CD

Easter Beagle & Friend—Pillow Set
Snoopy Pillow

Snoopy Pillow FABRICS AND SUPPLIES

Yardage

- ⅓ yard solid light blue for the sky
- ⅓ yard marbled medium green for the grass
- ⅛ yard light tan print for the trail
- ⅓ yard heavy white solid for Snoopy and the clouds
- ⅛ yard marbled yellow for the border and flowers
- ⅛ yard marbled dark purple for the border
- 1½ yards lavender gingham for the borders and pillow backing (¹⁄₁₆" or ⅛" checks)
- 1½ yards muslin for the background foundation and quilt backing
- 28" x 28" batting

Scraps

- Deep red for the roses
- Dark orange, aqua, light green, light orange, purple, pink, and yellow for the eggs, daisies, and foreground rosebushes
- Tan fabric for Easter basket (either a basket print or a suitably woven upholstery fabric)
- Medium purple and pink for Snoopy's bunny ears
- Black for Snoopy's ear, collar, and nose

Additional Supplies

- Fabric spray adhesive
- 3 yards ⅝" wide yellow rickrack
- Thin rope trim for the basket handle

Tubes of puffy craft paint in pink and bright blue

24" x 24" pillow form

4 – 9" x 12" sheets of Lite Steam-A-Seam 2

5 – 9" x 12" sheets of tracing paper

1 – 6" x 12" piece of transfer paper

4 – 3" x 3" pieces of wash-away stabilizer

6 – 9" x 12" sheets of tear-away stabilizer

Teflon pressing sheet

SNOOPY PILLOW
CUTTING AND ASSEMBLY

All cutting for the appliquéd area is done using the pattern pieces, which are already reversed; larger, background pieces are NOT reversed. Follow the instructions in chapter 2. Snoopy's eyes are satin stitched.

Background

1. The appliqué is layered on a 20" x 20" square of muslin. Cut a 12" x 18" piece of light blue sky fabric and place at the upper edge of the muslin, leaving a 1" edge of muslin extending around 3 sides. Hand baste the sky to the muslin.

2. Trace the pattern pieces for the foreground grass and the rose bush on the "not easy" liner of the fusible web. Remove the "easy" liner and adhere each piece to the wrong side of the appropriate fabric. Cut out the appliqué pieces, and transfer any remaining embroidery details. Set the rose bush aside. Using the quilt drawing on the CD as a guide, fuse the foreground grass to the background.

3. Trace the background grass and trail patterns onto tracing paper and use to cut out from the right side of medium green (grass) and the light tan print (trail). Adhere these pieces to the background with fabric adhesive spray, using the quilt drawing on the CD as a guide. Fuse the rose bush in the foreground (lower left side).

Snoopy and the Easter Basket

1. Follow the instructions in chapter 2 and create Snoopy's head, ear, and nose. If doubling of the fabric to prevent shadowing is necessary (page 15), do not use the heavy white fabric as the second fabric. Instead, use a thin white cotton or muslin. Snoopy's mouth lies on top of the outline of his head, so the mouth is always satin stitched after Snoopy's head is satin stitched to the background.

SNOOPY PILLOW assembly diagram

Fig. 1

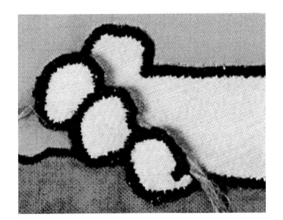

Fig. 2

2. For Snoopy's three-dimensional fingers that hold the basket:

    a. Cut 2 pieces of white fabric, approximately ¾" larger all around than the pattern for the fingers. Adhere the fabric pieces wrong sides together, using fabric adhesive spray. Trace the outline and details, and cut out the fingers.

    b. Layer the fingers between 4 layers of wash-away stabilizer (2 on top and 2 on the bottom). Using the pressing sheet, iron the stabilizer/fabric sandwich for a few seconds.

    c. Satin stitch around the edges and detail lines of the fingers using black thread. Soak the fingers in water to dissolve the stabilizer. Let dry.

3. Trace the pattern pieces for Snoopy's collar, body, foot, bunny ears, and tail on the "not easy" liner of the fusible web. Remove the "easy" liner and adhere each piece to the wrong side of the appropriate fabric. Cut out the appliqué pieces, and transfer any remaining embroidery details.

4. Using the pressing sheet, layer the pieces for Snoopy. Carefully press and allow to cool. Remove and adhere to the background, using the quilt drawing on the CD as a guide. Do not adhere the fingers on Snoopy's right paw at this point. The fingers will be attached along with the basket of eggs.

5. Working from the middle toward the outer edges, satin stitch Snoopy and the background details.

6. Trace the pattern pieces for the basket, eggs, daisies, roses, and clouds on the "not easy" liner of the fusible web. Remove the "easy" liner and adhere each piece to the wrong side of the appropriate fabric. Cut out the appliqué pieces. Arrange the eggs as shown (Fig. 1, page 44).

7. Layer the pieces using the pressing sheet. Press and allow to cool. Adhere the daisies and roses onto the background as shown. Create the eggs as shown. Complete the satin stitching within each egg before adhering to the background.

Note that there are 4 eggs in the basket, including a small piece of a purple one peeking out from behind the multicolored egg closest to Snoopy. This purple egg is decorated with dots of pink puffy paint. The middle, orange egg is decorated with dots of blue puffy paint. Follow the manufacturer's instructions.

8. Position the basket, basket rim, and eggs, carefully following figure 1 for placement. Cut a piece of the rope trim to use as the basket handle and check the length to make sure the handle reaches Snoopy's hand. Keeping the handle tucked under the corners of the basket, as shown, satin stitch the basket and eggs in place. Due to the thickness of the basket and eggs, it may be necessary to use dots of fabric glue to hold all the pieces down. The rest of the rope handle will still be hanging free.

9. Place Snoopy's fingers as shown (Fig. 2, page 44). Use dots of fabric glue to hold both the fingers and the rest of the basket handle in place. Tack down the fingers and the handle.

FINISHING

1. Square-up and trim the finished appliqué piece to measure 16½" x 16½".

2. For the borders (page 23), cut 2 yellow strips ¾" x the width of fabric (WOF) and add to the sides, top, and bottom.

3. Cut 2 lavender gingham strips 2¾" x WOF. Add to the sides, top, and bottom.

4. Cut 2 strips of marbled purple 2" x WOF. Add to the sides, top, and bottom.

5. Press the pillow top carefully from the wrong side. Layer with batting and a 28" x 28" square of muslin. Baste as needed. Quilt around the major elements and along the background lines and border edges. Square-up to measure 23½" x 23½".

6. Apply ⅝" wide yellow rickrack to the right side of the pillow top along the outside edge, so that curves of rickrack are at a ¼" seam line. Cut and overlap the rickrack at corners (Fig. 3).

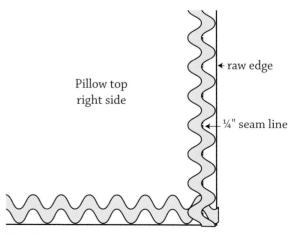

Fig. 3

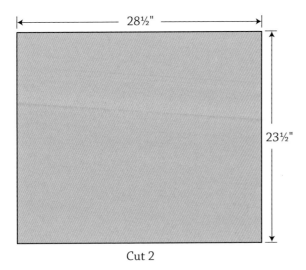

Cut 2

Fig. 4

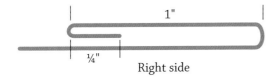

1"

¼"

Right side

Fig. 5. Turn the edge under ¼", then 1".

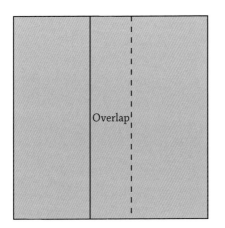

Overlap

Fig. 6. Overlap the two back pieces.

7. Cut 2 backing pieces 23½" x 28½" (Fig. 4).

8. Fold under ¼" along one 23½" edge of both backing sections and press. Then fold under another 1" and press (Fig. 5). Stitch along the folded edge.

9. Overlap and pin the 2 back sections to the front of the pillow, right sides together (Fig. 6). Baste inside ¼" seam allowance, and then stitch at ¼". Trim corners. Turn right-side out and press. Insert the pillow form. The pillow cover being slightly smaller than the pillow form ensures a snug fit.

EASTER BEAGLE & FRIEND—Pillow Set
WOODSTOCK PILLOW
24" x 24", made by the author
Full-size patterns on the CD

Easter Beagle & Friend—Pillow Set
Woodstock Pillow

Woodstock Pillow FABRICS AND SUPPLIES

Yardage
- ⅓ yard light blue solid for the sky
- ⅓ yard marbled medium green for the grass
- ⅛ yard marbled yellow for the borders
- 1½ yard lavender gingham for the borders and pillow backing (1/16" or ⅛" checks)
- ⅛ yard marbled dark purple for the border
- 1½ yards muslin for the background foundation and quilt backing
- 28" x 28" batting

Scraps
- 12" x 12" medium purple for the egg
- White for the clouds
- Light orange, dark orange, pink, and aqua for the egg
- Heavy solid yellow for Woodstock

Additional Supplies
- Fabric spray adhesive
- 3 yards ⅝" wide yellow rickrack
- Yellow embroidery thread
- 24" x 24" pillow form
- Teflon pressing sheet
- 3 – 9" x 12" sheets of Lite Steam-A-Seam 2
- 3 – 9" x 12" sheets of tracing paper
- 1 – 12" x 12" piece of transfer paper
- 6 – 9" x 12" sheets of tear-away stabilizer

WOODSTOCK PILLOW
CUTTING AND ASSEMBLY

All cutting for the appliquéd area is done using the pattern pieces and following the instructions in chapter 2. All patterns for appliqué pieces are already reversed; larger, background pieces are not reversed. Woodstock's eyes are satin stitched.

Background

1. The appliqué is layered on muslin. Cut a 20" x 20" square of muslin. Cut a 15" x 18" piece of light blue sky fabric. Place the sky fabric at top of the muslin, leaving 1" of muslin extending around 3 sides. Hand baste the sky to the muslin.

2. Trace the grass pattern and cut from the right side of the medium green for the grass. Adhere to the sky background with fabric adhesive spray, using the quilt drawing on the CD as a guide.

3. Trace the pattern pieces for the egg on the "not easy" liner of the fusible web. Remove the "easy" liner, and adhere each piece to the wrong side of the appropriate fabric. Cut out the appliqué pieces.

4. Using the pressing sheet, layer the pieces for the egg. Press and set aside.

Woodstock

1. In the same manner as Snoopy, create Woodstock using the solid yellow fabric. If doubling of the fabric to prevent shadowing is necessary (page 15), do not use the heavy yellow fabric as the second fabric. Instead, use a thin white cotton or muslin. Transfer all the detail lines onto Woodstock.

2. Create the clouds from white fabric.

3. Using the quilt drawing on the CD as a guide, adhere all pieces to the background.

4. Working from the middle toward the outer edges, satin stitch all elements. Transfer Woodstock's movement lines to the background and satin stitch. Satin stitch the outer edges of the feathers on his head with yellow thread.

FINISHING

Woodstock's pillow is bordered and finished in the same manner as Snoopy's pillow (pages 41–46).

WOODSTOCK PILLOW **assembly diagram**

RED, WHITE, AND BLUE—Bed Scarf

73" x 31", made by the author

Full-size patterns on the CD

Red, White, and Blue
Bed Scarf

FABRIC AND SUPPLIES

Yardage

- 5 yards solid red for Snoopy's clothing, the borders, Log Cabin blocks, backing and binding
- 2½ yards solid white for Snoopy's hat and the borders
- 2½ yards solid navy blue for the borders and Log Cabin blocks
- ¾ yard dark blue print for the sky
- ⅓ yard tan print for the sand
- ¼ yard gold metallic for the corner stars
- 39" x 81" batting

Scraps

- White flocked fabric for Snoopy
- Royal blue satin for the trim on Snoopy's clothes
- Black cotton for Snoopy's details
- Yellow flocked fabric for Woodstock

Additional Supplies

- Fabric spray adhesive
- Beige embroidery thread to coordinate with tan print (The thread should be slightly darker than the print.)
- Yellow embroidery thread for Woodstock's head
- 3 gold star buttons for Snoopy's hat
- 2 small gold beads for Snoopy's buttons
- Candy stick for Woodstock's flag pole
- Miniature American flag for Woodstock
- Metallic craft paint in squeeze bottles with tips: 4–6 shades in gold, silver, bright blue, and red.
- Glass seed beads to match paints
- White marking pencil
- Teflon pressing sheet
- 3 – 9" x 12" sheets of Lite Steam-A-Seam 2
- 5 – 9" x 12" sheets of tracing paper
- 1 – 12" x 12" piece of white transfer paper
- 1 – 12" x 12" piece of graphite transfer paper
- 4 – 6" x 6" pieces of wash-away stabilizer
- 12 – 9" x 12" sheets of tear-away stabilizer OR a 20" wide roll
- 15 sheets of your choice of paper-piecing foundation paper (optional: Perfect Paper Piecing Paper from www.debkarasik.com)

CUTTING AND ASSEMBLY

All cutting for the appliquéd area is done using the pattern pieces, which are already reversed; larger, background pieces are NOT reversed. Follow the instructions in chapter 2.

Assemble Snoopy and Woodstock appliqué elements one at a time. Note the special satin-stitching instructions for insertion of Snoopy's ear and Woodstock's flagpole. Snoopy's eyes are created of black fabric; Woodstock's eye is satin stitched.

Fig. 1

Snoopy

1. Create Snoopy's head (see pages 14–16). If doubling of the fabric to prevent shadowing is necessary (page 15), do not use the white, napped fabric as the second layer. Use a thin white cotton or muslin instead. Snoopy's mouth lies on top of the outline of his head, so satin stitch the mouth *after* satin stitching his head to the background.

2. To create Snoopy's ear, which hangs free, trace and cut out the ear pattern. Place this pattern on the wrong side of a small piece of black fabric, and using a white marking pencil, trace around the pattern. Place another piece of black fabric under the first, right sides together. Pin together, and with a shortened stitch length, sew the ears together on the white line. Leave the top edge open. Carefully clip all around the curved edge, turn, and press. Baste the ear closed on the top edge.

3. Trace all the remaining pattern pieces for Snoopy on the "not easy" liner of the fusible web. Remove the "easy" liner and adhere the appliqué pieces to the wrong side of the appropriate fabrics. Cut out the appliqué pieces and transfer any remaining embroidery details.

4. Using the pressing sheet, layer the pieces for Snoopy's jacket, sleeves, and hat. Layer these fused pieces and the belt with Snoopy's head, tail, and body. Insert the basted edge of Snoopy's ear under the rim of his hat (Fig. 1). Carefully fuse all pieces. Transfer any remaining detail lines onto the right side of Snoopy.

5. For each cuff and paw:

a. Create a sandwich by layering 2 pieces of the appropriate fabric (blue satin for the 2 cuffs, and white for the 2 paws), right sides out, with a layer of muslin between (Fig. 2).

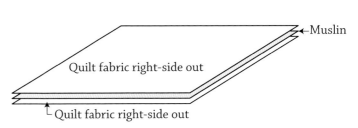

Quilt fabric right-side out

←—Muslin

⌐Quilt fabric right-side out

Fig. 2

b. Trace the cuff and paw patterns onto each sandwich using a disappearing marker. With a shortened stitch length, straight stitch around each outline. Coat the stitches lightly with seam sealant. Carefully cut out each shape just outside of the stitching line.

c. Keeping all pieces separate, layer and pin the 2 cuffs and 2 paws between 4 layers of water-soluble stabilizer (2 on top and 2 underneath). Press quickly, using a pressing cloth. Carefully satin stitch around each shape. Soak the shapes in water for a few minutes to dissolve the stabilizer. Allow them to dry and press lightly. Set aside.

Woodstock

1. Trace the pattern piece for Woodstock onto the "not easy" liner on the fusible web. If doubling the fabric to prevent shadowing (page 15), do not use the yellow fabric as the second layer. Use a thin white cotton or muslin instead.

2. Remove the "easy" liner and adhere to the wrong side of the yellow fabric. Cut out the appliqué piece and transfer any remaining details to the right side of the appliqué. Set aside.

BACKGROUND AND SATIN STITCHING

1. Cut a 20" x 28" piece of the blue sky fabric. Using white transfer paper, transfer detail lines for the fireworks in the upper sky area. Refer to the photo (page 50) for placement.

2. Trace the sand pattern onto tracing paper. Pin the pattern to the right side of the tan fabric. Cut, leaving approximately 2" of extra fabric extending all around the pattern edges to allow for shrinkage. Wet the fabric thoroughly with water, bunch it up horizontally, and secure all along the piece with rubber bands. Allow it to dry completely. Remove rubber bands and gently stretch the fabric open.

3. Using the same pattern, cut a piece of fusible interfacing to the size of the pattern. Pin the wrong side of the fabric to the fusible side of the interfacing. Press together with the tip of an iron, first along the top edge, and then only enough to adhere the fabric. Take care not to press out all of the pleats in the fabric. The pleating will create an extra textural effect in the foreground sand.

4. Lay the sky and sand piece over the quilt drawing; pin the sand in place as indicated. Carefully baste the sand to the sky piece, stitching close to the top edge of the sand piece. With beige embroidery thread and a wider setting, satin stitch the top edge of the sand in place. Transfer the detail lines to the sand. Decrease the stitch width, and satin stitch the detail lines on the sand.

5. Because Woodstock's flagpole is underneath his head and body, all his satin stitching must be completed before he is adhered to the background. Remove the remaining liner on Woodstock's fusible and adhere him to a layer of stabilizer. Pin to another layer of stabilizer. Complete all the satin stitching for Woodstock—black thread for the outlines and yellow thread for his feathers as shown.

NOTE

Using the candy stick as a flagpole is an embellishment choice that adds an adorable three-dimensional effect to the bed scarf. However, it adds quite a bit of difficulty to the completion of the piece. As an alternative, the flagpole can also be made from a piece of white grosgrain ribbon, or even a row of white satin stitching. The ribbon or stitching would simply be completed before Woodstock is adhered and satin stitched to the background, and the flag would be stitched on top of the pole.

6. Tear away the 2 layers of stabilizer beyond the satin stitching. Leave the stabilizer within Woodstock's body as needed, to stabilize him enough to stitch to the background.

7. Using the quilt drawing on the CD as a guide, place the appliqués on the background, with Snoopy to the left and Woodstock just to the right of the center. Fuse Snoopy's main body and head to the background, positioning him within the detail lines of the sand. Position Woodstock within the detail lines in the sand, and pin or use dots of glue to hold him in place.

8. Slide the flagpole under Woodstock as shown. Using black and yellow thread where needed, straight stitch Woodstock to the background through the satin-stitched edge.

9. Working from the middle areas toward the edges, satin stitch Snoopy to the background. Note that the back brim of Snoopy's hat curves under his ear. Slit the hat as noted on the pattern piece. Curve the satin stitching under and behind his ear as indicated in figure 1, page 52. Tack Snoopy's paws to the blue satin cuffs. Lay the paw/cuff units at the end of Snoopy's sleeves as shown and hold in place with dots of glue. Tack down at the corners of the cuffs and the tips of the paws.

10. To create Snoopy's bow tie:

a. Draw a 1½" circle on the wrong side of the red fabric. Place a second piece of the red fabric underneath it, right sides together. Pin.

b. Using a shortened stitch length, stitch around the circle. Cut out the circle approximately ⅛" beyond the stitching.

c. Pull the 2 pieces of fabric slightly apart and clip an opening in the center of the fabric on one side of the circle. Enlarge the clip to about ¾". Coat the clip with seam sealant.

d. Carefully turn the circle right-side out, shaping as needed.

e. Using a double strand of matching thread, hand stitch across the diameter of the circle (Fig. 3). Pull gently to gather. Knot to hold the gathers (Fig. 4).

f. Cut a small length of red fabric ¾" x 1¼". Sew right sides together along the length. Turn and press. Wrap the tube around the middle of the bow and tack in place. Tack the bowtie in place at Snoopy's neck, just above his paw (Fig. 5).

11. Create fireworks as follows:

a. Pin stabilizer in place behind the fireworks area. Using the drawing on the CD as a guide, draw in the lines of the fireworks with a white marking pencil. Embroider some of the lines in each burst in silver or gold threads, stitching over each embroidered line 2-3 times (Fig 6).

b. Apply silver and gold glitter paints to the larger background lines. Start paint lines at the center of the

Fig. 3

Fig. 4

Fig. 5

Fig. 6

Fig. 7

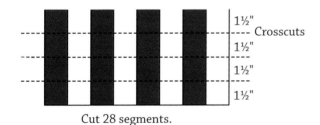

1½"
Crosscuts
1½"
1½"
1½"

Cut 28 segments.

Fig. 8

Join here

Remove

Remove

Fig. 9. Make 14.

fireworks bursts and work toward the outer edge. Allow it to dry. Apply a second coat. Before this second coat dries, press matching glass seed beads into the paint at approximately 1" intervals by hand. Use tweezers for easier placement.

c. When the second coat is dry, and again starting at the center and working outward, apply turquoise blue, light blue, and red glitter paints to the remaining lines, using the photos for guidance. Allow it to dry. Apply a second coat, pressing matching glass seed beads into the paint before it dries (Fig.7).

INNER BORDERS

1. Square-up and trim the finished panel to 18¼" x 26¼".

2. Border 1: Crosscut 3 solid blue strips ¾" x the width of fabric (WOF). Apply the top and bottom borders, then add the side borders (page 23).

3. Border 2 is strip-pieced.

a. Cut 4 red and 4 white 1½" x WOF strips (8 total). Make 1 strip-set with the 8 strips, alternating the red and white (Fig. 8). Press the seams toward the red strips.

b. Cut 28 segments 1½" wide with 8 squares in each segment.

c. Join the segments in pairs, alternating the position of the red and white squares. Remove the end squares as shown in figure 9. Make 14 pairs measuring 2½" x 7½".

d. Join 3 pairs together end-to-end, alternating the fabrics. Repeat to make a total of 4 sets of 3 pairs each.

e. Separate a four-square unit from the end of 2 of the sets for the shorter side borders.

f. Add the four-square units to the ends of the other 2 sets for the longer top and bottom borders.

g. Add the top and bottom borders first, then add the side borders, paying attention to the position of the red squares. Refer to the quilt photograph, page 50.

4. Border 3: Crosscut 4 solid blue strips 1¼" x WOF. Add to the top and bottom, then to the sides.

5. Border 4: Crosscut 4 white strips 3" x WOF. Measure both the length and width of the panel. Use 2 strips cut to the width measurement and add them to the sides.

6. Cut 4 white squares 4" x 4".

7. Trace 4 pattern pieces for the small stars pattern on the "not easy" liner of the fusible web. Remove the "easy" liner and adhere each piece of fusible web to the wrong side of the gold fabric. Fuse the gold stars to the white squares, centering the stars on the squares. Stitch around the edges of the stars with gold thread and a narrow zigzag stitch. Carefully trim the squares to 3" x 3", keeping each gold star centered.

8. Cut the remaining 3" strips to the measurement of the top and bottom blue borders PLUS ½". Add the star squares to both ends of the strips and add to the top and bottom of the panel.

9. Border 5 is applied to the sides only. Crosscut 2 solid blue strips 1¼" x WOF. Add to the sides.

LOG CABIN BLOCKS

Three rows of red, white, and blue Log Cabin blocks are added to both ends of the center panel. These blocks are foundation-pieced on either paper or a tear-away stabilizer. You need 10 red and white (R/W) blocks, 10 blue and white (B/W) blocks, and 10 blue and red (B/R) blocks to complete the bed scarf.

Each Log Cabin block uses slightly less than one full strip of each color, but do not discard the strip leftovers. They can be used in subsequent blocks.

Work row by row, cutting the fabric for each row, then piecing the blocks in that row. To make both row#1 units (one for each end of the appliqué panel), cut strips as follows:

6 – 1½" x WOF blue strips
8 – 1½" x WOF red strips
6 – 1½" x WOF white strips

While all strips for the subsequent rows can be cut at the same time (which would require one full strip for each color per block resulting in 14 more blue and white strips, and 12 more red strips), I prefer to cut as I go, which allows for using the strip leftovers and cutting fewer total strips.

1. Make 30 copies of the block pattern on your choice of foundation material.

2. Cut 3 strips 1¼" x WOF from the red, white, and blue fabrics (9 total).

3. The piecing chart on page 59 indicates how the colors are placed in each Log Cabin block. For example, in the Red & White blocks, piece #1 is red, piece #2 is white, and so on. Refering to the chart, piece the Log Cabin blocks as follows:

    a. Hold a foundation up to a light with the marked side facing you. With the color indicated for #1, cut a piece of fabric that will cover shape #1 and position it on the unmarked side with about ¼" of fabric extending all around. This piece of fabric may be held in place with a small dot of fabric glue if desired.

    b. With the color indicated for #2, cut and place fabric to cover shape #2, right sides together with shape #1. Carefully fold fabric #2 out to make sure it will adequately cover shape #2.

    c. Fold the fabric back into position. Carefully pin the fabrics together from the marked side of the foundation.

    d. With a shortened stitch length, stitch on the marked side of the foundation (stitching through the foundation to the fabric on the other side), along the line that falls between shapes #1 and #2. Begin and end stitching 2 – 3 stitches beyond the end of the line. Trim the seam if needed.

    e. Turn the foundation over and unfold fabric #2, creasing it open.

    f. Using the same procedure, measure and cut fabric to cover shape #3, and so on.

4. Arrange the completed blocks into 6 rows of 5 blocks each, with the vertical rows closest to the appliqué panel counting as Row #1, the middle rows as Row #2, and the outside rows as Row #3. See the chart on page 60 and refer to the photographs in figures 10 and 11 for guidance. Notice that the blocks in matching rows are the same but oriented differently from each other.

5. Sew the blocks into rows, join the rows into 2 panels of 3 rows each, and add to the sides of the appliqué panel.

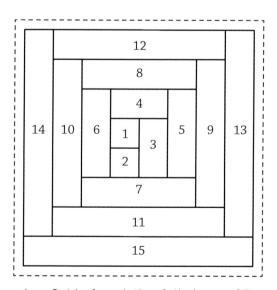

Log Cabin foundation full-size on CD

PIECING CHART

Make 10 Red & White	Make 10 Blue & White	Make 10 Blue & Red
#1 – Red	#1 – White	#1 – Blue
#2 – White	#2 – Blue	#2 – Red
#3 – Whitc	#3 – Blue	#3 – Red
#4 – Red	#4 – White	#4 – Blue
#5 – White	#5 – Blue	#5 – Red
#6 – Red	#6 – White	#6 – Blue
#7 – White	#7 – Blue	#7 – Red
# 8 – Red	#8 – White	#8 – Blue
#9 – White	#9 – Blue	#9 – Red
#10 – Red	#10 – White	#10 – Blue
#11 – White	#11 – Blue	#11 – Red
#12 – Red	#12 – White	#12 – Blue
#13 – White	#13 – Blue	#13 – Red
#14 – Red	#14 – White	#14 – Blue
#15 – White	#15 – Blue	#15 – Red

Row #3 Row #2 Row #1

Fig. 10

Row #1 Row #2 Row #3

Fig. 11

Row #3	Row #2	Row #1	Appliqué Panel	Row #1	Row #2	Row #3
R/W	B/W	B/R		B/R	B/W	R/W
B/W	B/R	R/W		R/W	B/R	B/W
B/R	R/W	B/W		B/W	R/W	B/R
R/W	B/W	B/R		B/R	B/W	R/W
B/W	B/R	R/W		R/W	B/R	B/W

FINISHING

1. From the back, carefully press the entire quilt in an up-and-down motion, taking care not to stretch it.

2. Cut 6 blue strips 1¼" x WOF. Add them to the sides, then to the top and bottom.

3. Make a backing 39" x 81" from the solid red. Layer the quilt top with the backing and batting. Baste as needed. Quilt around the characters and main elements . Using a brush-out marker, draw 5 or 6 small stars on the background sky and quilt with gold thread. See the quilt drawing on the CD for guidance. Quilt in the ditch along each border and between the Log Cabin squares. Additional quilting may be done within the Log Cabin blocks if desired.

4. Carefully trim the batting and backing even with the top of the quilt. Cut 6 – 2¼" x WOF red strips. Join end-to-end. Fold in half lengthwise, right sides together, and press. Apply binding to the top and bottom and then to the sides (page 24).

5. Glue a mini-flag to Woodstock's flagpole. Stitch 3 gold star buttons to Snoopy's hatband and 1 small gold bead to each of his sleeve cuffs.

6. Create 4 gold stars for the corners. On the wrong side of a small piece of gold fabric, trace 4 large star patterns. Pin to a second piece of gold, right sides together. With a shortened stitch length, stitch around the tracing line. Trim the fabric to ⅛" around the traced line. Clip the corners and points. On the back side, make a small slit in the fabric, taking care not to clip through to the front fabric. Turn carefully and coat the slit with seam sealant. Press. Tack 1 star to each corner.

NOTE

If a longer drape is desired over the edge of the bed, simply add more rows of Log Cabin blocks, maintaining the pattern created. For example, the next row added would be a Row #1, then Row #2, and so on.

AUTUMN LEAF JUMP—Bed Quilt

70" x 86", made by the author

Full-size patterns on the CD

Autumn Leaf Jump
Bed Quilt

Due to the size of AUTUMN LEAF JUMP and the need for quilting in the inner, appliquéd area, the quilt is made and quilted in sections. This will be explained more fully within the directions that follow.

FABRICS AND SUPPLIES

Yardage

- 1½ yards of light blue for the sky background
- ½ yard of white for Snoopy and the clouds
- ⅛ yard of black for Snoopy's ears and details
- 3 yards of navy blue for the inner border and binding
- 3 yards of marbled yellow for the straight border, diamond border, striped border, and leaves
- 3 yards of medium blue for the inner and outer borders
- 6⅛ yards backing
- 79" x 104" batting

For Leaves, Woodstock, and Pieced Borders

- ¾ yard dark yellow
- 1 yard bright yellow
- ¾ yard gold
- ¾ yard bright orange
- ¾ yard bright red
- ¾ yard magenta
- ¾ yard dark green
- ¾ yard bright green
- ¾ yard moss green
- ¾ yard dark rust
- ¾ yard medium rust
- ¾ yard medium brown
- ¾ yard medium blue

Additional Supplies

- Fabric spray adhesive
- Teflon pressing sheet
- 25 – 9" x 12" sheets of Lite Steam-A-Seam 2 OR 24" x 4½ yards
- 1 – 5-yard roll of 36" wide tracing paper OR 4 – 19" x 24" sheets
- 1 – 12" x 12" piece of transfer paper
- 13 – 9" x 12" sheets of tear-away stabilizer OR 1 – 20"-wide roll

CUTTING AND ASSEMBLY CENTER SECTION

All cutting for the appliqués is done using the pattern pieces and following the instructions in chapter 2. Note that larger appliqué pieces are NOT reversed, and should be applied with fabric adhesive spray. Snoopy's eye is created of fabric; Woodstock's eye is satin stitched.

Background

1.   Cut a piece of light blue sky fabric 33" x 49" for the background.

2.   Make a tracing of the quilt drawing (full size on the CD) to place over the sky background to help with placement of the appliqué pieces. Because of the size of the appliqués, some pieces will be layered directly on the background without using a pressing sheet.

Snoopy and Clouds

Snoopy's head and body and the clouds are applied with adhesive spray (these patterns are not reversed). The rest of the appliqué pieces are reversed and applied with double-sided fusible web.

1.   Trace the patterns for Snoopy's head, body, and the clouds on the CD and cut from the right side of the white fabric. Spray with adhesive spray and adhere to the sky, following the quilt drawing on the CD. Do not permanently adhere yet.

2.   Trace the pattern pieces for Snoopy's ears, eye, nose, collar, arm, tail, and spots on

the "not easy" side of the fusible web. Remove the other "easy" liner and adhere each piece to the wrong side of the appropriate fabric. Cut out the appliqué pieces and transfer any remaining embroidery details.

3.   Layer the pieces for Snoopy and the clouds on the sky background fabric, using the quilt drawing on the CD for correct placement. Press to adhere all pieces in place.

Woodstock

1.   Trace the pattern pieces for Woodstock onto the "not easy" liner on the fusible web. Remove the "easy" liner and adhere to the wrong side of the bright yellow fabric. Cut out the appliqué pieces and transfer any remaining details. Double the fabric to prevent shadowing if necessary (page 15).

2.   Using the quilt drawing on the CD for correct placement, position Woodstock on the sky as indicated and fuse in place.

Leaf Pile

1.   For each of the 13 leaf fabrics, use a separate piece of double-sided fusible web. Use the photos as a guide in the placement of the fabrics. Yellows are scattered throughout and all over the pile, so make more of them. There is no pattern for the shape of the leaves. Cut about 135 irregular shapes with a variety of different angles approximately 1" x 2" or 2" x 2" (The total will depend on the sizes and shapes that you cut.) See figures 1 and 2, page 64.

Fig. 1

Fig. 2

2. To make the leaves, remove the "easy" liner from the fusible web and adhere the fusible to the wrong side of one of the leaf fabrics. On the remaining "not easy" liner, trace shapes for numerous leaves. Cut the leaves out on the tracing lines and remove the remaining paper liner. You may find it helpful to keep the fabrics grouped by color on trays or in piles.

3. Lay out the leaf pile at the bottom of the sky fabric. Note that the darker colors are concentrated on the bottom of the leaf pile and behind other leaves. The colors lighten toward the top of the pile. Other than these guidelines, don't stress as to the placement of the leaves! Use the quilt photograph as a guide (page 61). Arrange and rearrange until you are happy with the result, keeping the top edge of the leaf pile 4"–5" below Snoopy, and sloping the pile down toward each side. When the pile is "leaf-y" enough, press and fuse the leaves in place.

4. Using the pattern drawing as a guide, mark the movement lines on the sky for Snoopy and Woodstock. Also, lightly transfer the wind lines for quilting. Then, working from the middle toward the edges, satin stitch the characters and detail lines.

5. The satin stitching on the leaf pile will take some time. Do not rush. Stitch the leaves in the background of the pile first, then move out to the leaves toward the front of the pile, finishing a section at a time.

6. Square up and trim the piece to 29½" x 44½". Cut 5 navy blue strips 1¼" x the width of fabric (WOF), piecing as needed. Apply to sides of the center section, then to the top and bottom (page 23).

7. Cut 2 length-of-fabric (LOF) 5" x 46" yellow strips and 2 LOF 5" x 39" yellow strips. Apply to the sides, then to the top and bottom. Note: Although the finished border will only be 4" wide, cutting the strips a little wider allows for an easy application of the Double Chain of Squares border.

8. Carefully press from the wrong side, taking care not to stretch. On a large, flat surface, lay out 54" x 94" pieces of backing, wrong-side up, and batting. Center the quilt top so the batting and backing extend 7" beyond the quilt top on the sides and 20" beyond on both the top and bottom. The batting and backing are sized to fit the middle portion of the quilt (under the appliquéd area) from the finished top to the finished bottom. Baste the batting and backing together within the appliquéd area and along the narrow navy blue border (Fig. 3).

9. Quilt around the characters and main elements. Quilt along the top edge of the leaf pile and inside the pile, following the lines of the leaves throughout so that quilting is completed at a minimum of 4"–5" intervals. Finally, quilt along the inner edge of the navy blue border.

10. Remove the basting from the border area. Turn the quilt over; from the wrong side, fold all the batting and backing over so that they lie on the back of the quilted area. Pin or baste loosely into place. With the batting and backing

Fig. 3

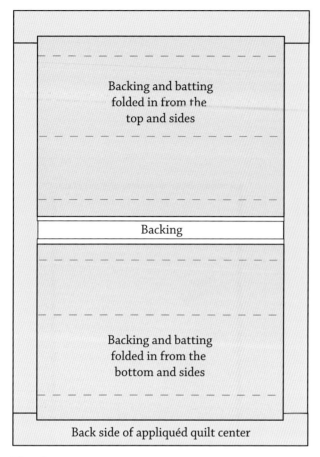

Backing and batting
folded in from the
top and sides

Backing

Backing and batting
folded in from the
bottom and sides

Back side of appliquéd quilt center

Fig. 4

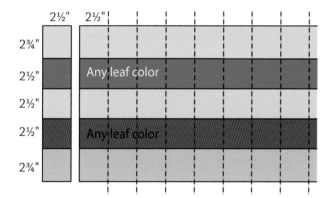

Fig. 5. Make 12. Cut 84.

folded to the back, they will remain out of the way for the rest of the sewing, and will later be unpinned and quilted with additional lengths of batting and backing attached on each side (Fig. 4).

CUTTING AND ASSEMBLY—OUTER SECTION

Double Chain of Squares Border

This border helps to emphasize the leaves and acts as a transition between the yellow and blue borders. Note that the marbled yellow border can be adjusted (slightly and in equal amounts on opposite sides) to fit the Double Chain of Squares.

1. Cut strips for the Double Chain of Squares border according to the chart below.

2. Make 12 strip-sets as shown in figure 5, varying the leaf color strips. Press the seams all in one direction. Cut 7 – 2½" segments from each strip-set (total 84; you might have a few extra).

Double Chain of Squares Border		
Fabric	**2¾" x 18"**	**2½" x 18"**
marbled yellow	12 strips	12 strips
assorted leaf color fabrics	none	24 strips
medium blue	12 strips	none

3. Divide the segments into 2 roughly equal piles, one for strips that are darker and one for strips that are lighter. Some of the pieces may not fit easily into either a lighter or darker category, and that's fine. Just place these pieces into the most similar of the 2 piles.

4. Take the dark pile and *carefully* re-press the seams on the pieces flat, then press so the seam allowances face in the opposite direction (Fig. 6).

5. Take one segment from each pile and place right sides together, offsetting the light segment by one square. Stitch and carefully press the new seam open (Fig. 7).

6. Sew all the dark and light segments into pairs, then sew them into sets of 4, and so on, to make the 4 borders (Fig. 8, page 68).

- ❧ For the 46" side borders, you need about 23 segments. Make 2.

- ❧ For the 39" top and bottom borders, you need about 17 segments. Make 2.

7. Sew the longer borders to the sides of the quilt top along the yellow squares sides so that the points of the leaf-colored squares fall just at the seam line with the yellow border, creating a 4" finished border of the yellow. Then add the the top and bottom borders, again creating a 4" finished yellow border (Fig. 9, page 69). Slightly trim the marbled yellow, if needed, for the correct length. Make sure any trimming is identical on the opposite sides of the quilt. Begin and end the stitching approximately 2" in from the corners.

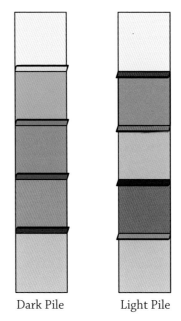

Dark Pile   Light Pile

Fig. 6

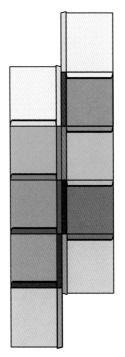

Fig. 7

Fig. 8

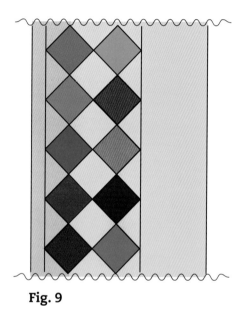

Fig. 9

8. After applying the Double Chain of Squares borders to all 4 sides, carefully fold back and pin the loose ends so that the squares meet and align at the corners, forming a miter. Finish stitching the 2" at each end of the yellow borders from the end of the previous stitching to the corners. Then stitch the miter from the inner corner to the outer edge of the quilt (Fig. 9).

Alternate Method – OK. So you have been trying to accomplish finishing up these corners for hours, and the squares and corners are not matching up. What to do? There is an alternative, although I am not sure it would be considered a true quilting method by those dedicated to the craft! But, the good news? This method is guaranteed to work. You will work on one corner of the quilt at a time.

a. Find the blindstitch or the blind hemstitch on your machine (referring to your machine's manual). Adjust your sewing machine so the zigzag part of the stitch is very narrow—less than ⅛" and closer to ¹⁄₁₆".

b. Thread the top of the machine with clear thread. Loosen the top tension, if necessary, to ensure that the bobbin thread does not pull up to the top.

c. Lay the quilt right-side up, so that the top right corner is completely flat. Position the top and side borders so that the top border lies flat on top of the side border. Carefully pin under a diagonal seam allowance of the top border so that the squares of the top border match and align with the squares of the side border and the whole corner area lies flat. At the same time, pin under the seam allowances of the marbled yellow border. Ensure that everything is lying flat.

d. Using the blind hemstitch and sewing on the top side of the quilt, first sew the open seam areas between the marbled yellow borders and the Double Chain of Squares borders, sewing from the middle of the quilt toward the corner. Finally, stitch from the inner corner toward the outer corner, along the diagonal seam between the side and top border sections (Fig. 11).

e. Repeat for the remaining three corners. Press the corners at a low temperature, taking care not to melt the clear thread.

9. To finish the Double Chain of Squares border, cut 5 strips of the medium blue fabric 1¼" x WOF. Apply to the sides of the quilt, then to the top and bottom, piecing as needed. From the wrong side of the quilt, trim the excess blue and yellow points along the border seams. Note: You could trim the excess points from the borders before adding them to the quilt, but you will need to handle the bias edges carefully to ensure they don't stretch.

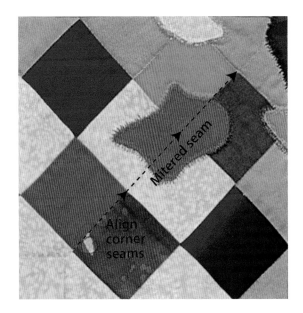

Fig. 10

Fig. 11

Striped Border

Like the leaves, color placement in the striped border is random. It is made of strips of varying widths. This element will emphasize the fun, unplanned theme of the quilt.

Use the same fabrics you used to make the leaves and the Double Chain of Squares border.

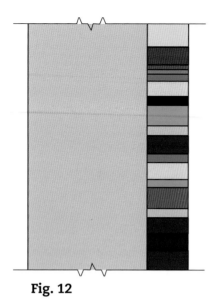

Fig. 12

Fig. 13

1. Cut strips from the fabric leftovers, cutting random numbers of strips in the following widths: 2", 1½", 1¼", 1", and ¾". Don't worry about having the same number of each color, or the same number of a certain width. Remember, the randomness of this border is the key. Don't over think it. The finished border will have a fun, scrappy look!

2. Make piles of similar strips—by color or value, whichever you feel works best. For example, make piles of lights, darks, and mediums; or piles of all the yellows, all the greens, all the reds, etc. Selecting pieces from the different piles, sew randomly together in strip-sets of 3–4 to 8–10 strips in each—in whatever combination of strips is comfortable for you. Press the seams in one direction, taking care not to stretch them out of shape. Crosscut segments from the strip-sets 3" wide. You need approximately 300" of segments.

4. Note that the striped border and the wide medium blue border adjacent to it are created in one unit with plain cornerstones at the corners.

    a. Measure the length and width of the quilt top.

    b. From the medium blue, cut 2 LOF strips 7½" x the length measurement and 2 LOF strips 7½" x the width measurement.

    c. Make 4 pieced striped borders of the 3" strip-set segments to match the measurements of the 4 medium blue strips.

    d. Join the blue and striped border strips (Fig. 12).

e. Add the blue and striped side borders to the quilt top (Fig. 13).

f. Cut 4 squares of medium blue 10" x 10". Add to both ends of the top and bottom borders. Add to the quilt.

Scattered Leaves

The corners of the quilt are covered with a scattering of 26 leaves, made from the same fabrics as both the leaves in the pile and the Double Chain of Squares border. There are 5 different leaf patterns on the CD, each made in several different fabrics.

With each leaf pattern are suggestions for the number to make of specific fabrics; however, you should feel free to experiment and play with the colors and placements. Darker leaves should be layered underneath brighter leaves. Other than that, there are no real rules; your leaves can be scattered in any manner you wish. Use a variety of each color.

1. <u>**Leaf #1**</u> – Make 7 for each corner (a total of 28). Color suggestions:
   - 3 of bright yellow/light orange
   - 4 of medium rust/dark orange
2. <u>**Leaf #2**</u> – Make 4 for each corner (a total of 16). Color suggestions:
   - 2 of medium rust/dark orange
   - 2 of dark purple/maroon
3. <u>**Leaf #3**</u> – Make 2 for each corner (a total of 8). Color suggestions:
   - 1 of medium rust/dark orange
   - 1 of dark maroon/purple

4. <u>**Leaf #4**</u> – Make 2 for each corner (a total of 8). Color suggestions:
   - 1 of medium rust/dark orange
   - 1 of dark purple/maroon
5. <u>**Leaf #5**</u> – Make 11 for each corner (a total of 44). Color suggestions:
   - 5 of bright yellow/light orange
   - 4 of medium rust/dark orange
   - 2 of dark brown/maroon/purple

6. To create this number of leaves, an assembly line approach is efficient. So, you may wish to perform all the tracing at once, then the fusing, then the stitching, and so forth. For each leaf:

   a. Trace the patterns for the 5 different leaf shapes in the numbers indicated for each shape on the "not easy" liner

Fig. 14. Upper corner

of the fusible web. Remove the "easy" liner and adhere each piece to the wrong side of the appropriate fabric. Cut out the leaves and transfer any remaining embroidery details.

b. Using the quilt photo (page 61) as a guide, arrange the leaves on one corner of the quilt at a time. Press the leaves carefully to adhere to the quilt top. An example of a leaf arrangement is provided on the CD.

c. With stabilizer under the quilt top and behind the leaves, attach the leaves, with a free-motion, narrow zigzag stitch, dropping the feed dogs and using a machine quilting or embroidery foot so you don't have to repeatedly turn the quilt as you're stitching. Use thread to match each leaf. Stitch around each leaf a second time with a denser zigzag stitch (Fig. 15).

Fig. 15. Free-motion machine embroidery holds the leaves.

FINISHING

On the wrong side of the quilt, the batting and backing will still be pinned up under the appliquéd area. Lay the quilt wrong-side up on a flat surface and unpin the layers. Smooth out the sections of the batting and backing.

Attach additional batting and backing to the sides as follows:

1. Cut 2 pieces of backing and 2 pieces of batting 20½" x 94" (Fig. 16).

2. Continue working from the back side. Pin the backing toward the center of the quilt and away from the edge of the batting. Carefully turn the quilt over and pin the quilt top away from the edge of the batting (Fig 17).

3. You can join the additional pieces of batting to the sides by hand or, since the batting seam will fall under the double chain of squares border, with a machine seam (Fig. 17, page 73).

a. To join by hand, place the batting pieces next to each other and whipstitch together. Use pieces of tape along the joining line to hold the batting together until the stitching is complete (Fig. 18, page 74).

b. To join by machine, layer the batting pieces so that they overlap by about 1". Hold together with straight pins; stitch together with a long, wide zigzag (Fig. 19, page 74).

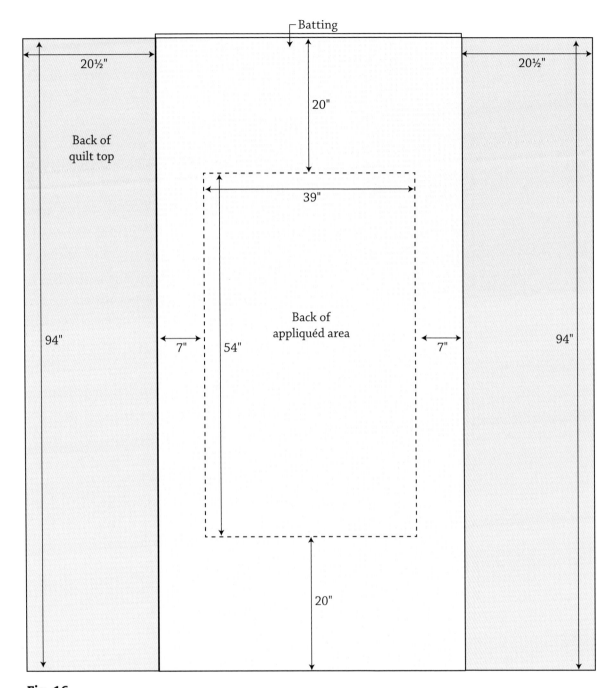

Fig. 16

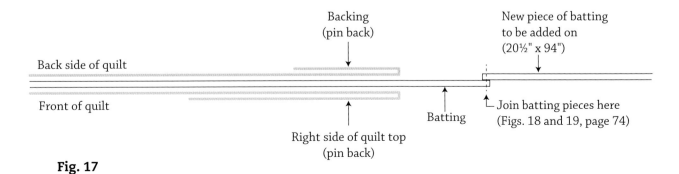

Fig. 17

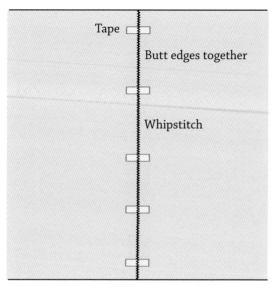

Tape

Butt edges together

Whipstitch

Fig. 18

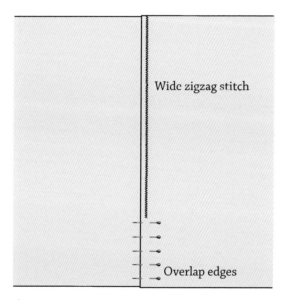

Wide zigzag stitch

Overlap edges

Fig. 19

5. After both sides of the batting are joined, fold the new batting piece over to the front with the quilt top. Then, layer 2 pieces of backing fabric, right sides together, and seam. Complete the opposite side in the same manner. You will now have a complete quilt of 3 layers, with the appliquéd area already fully quilted (Fig. 20).

6. Lay the quilt flat, right-side up, and baste the remaining outer areas together. Quilt the outer areas, including on each side of the Double Chain of Squares border, along both edges of this border, and around all of the leaves.

7. Carefully trim the batting and backing even with the quilt top. To create the binding, cut 9 – 2¼" x WOF strips of navy blue. Apply to the side edges, and then the top and bottom edges.

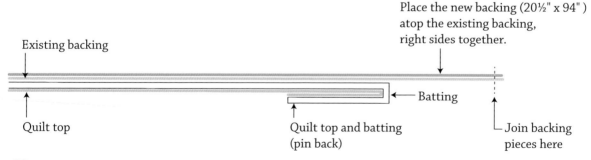

Place the new backing (20½" x 94") atop the existing backing, right sides together.

Existing backing

Quilt top

Batting

Quilt top and batting (pin back)

Join backing pieces here

Fig. 20

It's the Great Pumpkin
Table Topper
26½" x 26½", made by the author
Full-size patterns on the CD

It's the Great Pumpkin
Table Topper

FABRIC AND SUPPLIES

Yardage

- ½ yard dark blue sky print for the background sky
- ⅓ yard medium brown wood print for the fence
- ½ yard marbled medium green for the middle-ground leaves and border
- ½ yard medium orange for the pumpkins and borders
- ½ yard black for Franklin's hair, the borders, and bats
- ¼ yard pink for Linus's and Sally's skin
- ⅛ yard light green for the foreground leaves
- ⅛ yard light orange for the foreground pumpkin
- 1 yard of muslin
- ⅞ yard backing
- 28½" x 28½" batting

Scraps

- Black for Franklin's hair
- Medium brown for Franklin's skin
- Dark purple for Franklin's shirt
- Medium blue for Linus's shirt
- Dark pink for Sally's shirt
- Bright yellow for Sally's hair
- Marbled medium yellow for the moon

Additional Supplies

- Spray fabric adhesive
- Machine embroidery thread in yellow, silver, and gold
- Teflon pressing sheet
- 9 – 9" x 12" sheets of Lite Steam-A-Seam 2 OR 1¼ yards 24" wide
- 2 – 19" x 24" sheets of tracing paper
- 1 – 12" x 48" piece of transfer paper
- 16 – 9" x 12" sheets of tear-away stabilizer OR 1 – 20" wide roll

TABLE TOPPER CUTTING AND ASSEMBLY

All cutting for the appliquéd area is done using the pattern pieces and following the instructions in chapter 2. Assemble one appliqué element at a time. All patterns for appliqué pieces are already reversed; the fence and larger background pieces are NOT reversed and will be applied with spray adhesive. The character s' eyes are created of freehand machine embroidery.

Background

The appliquéd area of the table topper piece is layered on muslin.

1. Cut a 36" x 36" of muslin. Cut a 13" x 26" piece of dark blue sky fabric. Place the sky fabric at the top of the muslin, leaving 5" of muslin extending at the top and sides. Hand baste the sky to the muslin.

2. Trace the fence pattern onto tracing paper, pin to the right side of the wood print fabric, and cut out. Lightly coat the top edge of the fence piece with seam sealant. Using the pattern drawing as a guide, position the wood print on top of the sky and machine baste in place at the top edge of the fence. Baste as close to the top edge of the fence as possible.

3. Trace the pattern pieces for the dark green leaves (appearing behind Linus) on the "not easy" liner of the fusible web. Remove the "easy" liner, and adhere to the wrong side of the dark green fabric. Cut out the leaves and transfer the details. Using the quilt drawing on the CD

as a guide, carefully press leaves onto the fence background.

Linus

1. Make Linus's head and mouth; then add them to the background before adding his hair. Double the skin fabric if shadowing occurs (page 15). Note that his hair falls both on his forehead and onto the background fabric. Accordingly, transfer the hair lines onto his head and, after his head is adhered to the background, complete the transfer of the lines onto the background behind him. After all of the hair lines are properly transferred, complete the satin stitching on the hair.

2. Trace the pattern pieces for Linus's shirt, arms, and pumpkin on the "not easy" liner of the fusible web. (Note that the arms may have to be doubled to prevent shadowing.) Remove the "easy" liner and adhere the fusible web to the wrong side of the appropriate fabrics. Cut out the appliqué pieces and transfer any remaining details.

3. Layer all of Linus's pieces, including his pumpkin, using the pressing sheet. Fuse all the pieces and allow to cool. Carefully remove from the pressing sheet and, using the quilt drawing on the CD as a guide, layer the appliqué pieces on the background, nestling in between the leaves.

4. Trace the pattern pieces for the medium green leaves in the center of the appliquéd area (between Sally and Franklin) on the "not easy" liner of the fusible web as indicated. Remove the

"easy" liner, transfer the details, and adhere the medium green leaves in front of Linus.

Franklin

1. Create Franklin's head.

2. Trace the pattern pieces for Franklin's hair, shirt, hand, and pumpkin on fusible web. Create the appliqués and transfer the remaining details. Layer on the pressing sheet, press, and allow to cool. Remove and adhere to the background, using the quilt drawing on the CD as a guide.

Sally

1. Make Sally's head. Her topknot of hair is extensively embroidered. It should be created in the same way as the character's faces. It will be much easier to embroider the topknot if the embroidery is completed before adhering this piece to the rest of the hair.

2. Trace the pattern pieces for the rest of Sally's hair, shirt, arms, leaf, and pumpkin on the fusible web. Create the appliqués and transfer the remaining details. Layer on the pressing sheet, press, and allow to cool. Remove and adhere to the background, using the pattern drawing as a guide.

Foreground Pumpkin/Leaves

Trace the pattern pieces for the foreground leaves and pumpkin. Create the appliqués and transfer the remaining details. Layer on the pressing sheet as needed, press, and allow to cool. Remove and adhere to the background, using the quilt drawing on the CD as a guide.

Moon and Bats

Trace the pattern pieces of the moon and bats on the "not easy" liner of the fusible web as described in Chapter 2. Layer on the pressing sheet as needed, press, and allow to cool. Remove the "not easy" liner and adhere to the background sky, using the quilt drawing on the CD as a guide.

FINISHING

1. Working from the middle out toward the edges, satin stitch the characters and detail lines. Satin stitch the moon with yellow thread. Satin stitch the bats with silver/black metallic thread. To create the rougher, unkempt edges of Franklin's hair, lower the feed dogs and straight stitch around and just inside the raw edges. Then meander throughout the hair to give it a curly appearance (Fig. 1).

Fig. 1

2. Place the table topper face down on a heavy towel and press carefully. Trim to measure 23½" x 23½".

3. To create the borders (page 23):

    a. Crosscut 4 medium orange strips ¾" x width of fabric (WOF), piecing as needed. Apply to the sides, then to the top and bottom.

The remaining borders have a cornerstone, so the border strips can be sewn into one unit and then applied to the quilt.

    b. Crosscut 4 marbled medium green strips 1½" x WOF.

    c. For the orange and black striped border, crosscut 3 black and 3 orange strips 2⅜" x WOF and 1 orange strip 3" x WOF. Cut the strips in half, making each approximately 20" long.

    d. Make a 13-strip strip-set, starting and ending with the wider orange strips, alternating the orange and black. (You'll have one extra 2⅜" orange strip.) The slightly wider strip at each end will allow for some "fudging" with the total length—that is, if the measurements of the quilt top are not exact or cannot be exactly divisible by the number of black and orange strips, there is some room for adjustment at the ends. This is especially useful as the orange and black border is used in both the tablemat and the placemat, though the sides of the pieces vary in length.

    e. Crosscut 4–1" segments from the strip-set and sew to the 4 marbled medium green strips to make 4 border strips. Trim the excess green fabric. (Save the remaining strip-set for the placemat border.)

    f. Measure the sides of the quilt AND the top and bottom width of the quilt. Trim the border strips to those measurements. Add borders to the top and bottom.

    g. Cut 4 black squares 2" x 2" and sew 1 square to each end of the remaining border strips and add to the sides (Fig. 2).

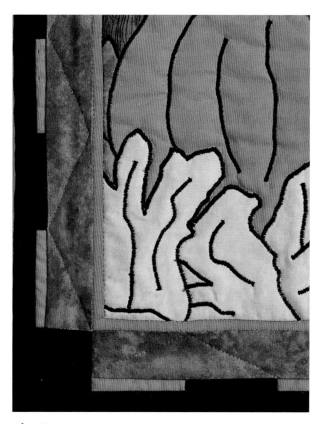

Fig. 2.

4. Press the quilt top again from the wrong side. Square-up and trim the edges and corners evenly.

5. Cut a piece of backing 28½" x 28½". Layer with the batting and quilt top and baste as needed. Quilt around the characters and main elements, and within the borders as shown in figure 2 (page 79). Using a brush-out fabric marker, trace several small stars scattered throughout the sky. See the quilt drawing on the CD for guidance. Machine embroider the stars with gold metallic thread.

6. Cut 4 black strips 2¼" x WOF for the binding. Keeping the black and orange border at ¼" wide, apply the binding (page 24).

Table topper assembly diagram

IT'S THE GREAT PUMPKIN
Placemat
18" x 12", made by the author
Full-size patterns on the CD

It's the Great Pumpkin
Placemat

Yardage
- ¼ yard of medium purple for the background sky
- ½ yard of medium orange for the background fog and border
- ½ yard of black for Snoopy and the foreground, border, and binding
- ¼ yard of medium green for the border
- ½ yard of muslin foundation
- ½ yard backing
- 14" x 20" batting

Scraps
- Marbled medium yellow for moon

Additional Supplies
- Fabric spray adhesive
- Machine embroidery thread in yellow, silver, and gold
- Teflon pressing sheet
- 1 – 19" x 24" sheet of tracing paper
- 1 – 12" x 16" piece of transfer paper
- 4 – 9" x 12" sheets of tear-away stabilizer

PLACEMAT CUTTING AND ASSEMBLY

The pattern pieces for the placemat are not reversed. All pattern pieces should be placed on the right side of the fabric and cut out. As with the tablemat, the pieces are applied to a muslin foundation.

1. Cut a muslin foundation 14" x 20". Using the pattern pieces, cut the sky, smoke, Snoopy/foreground, and moon. Using the pattern drawing as a guide, place the purple sky on the muslin and hand baste in place, leaving a 2" border of muslin all around the piece.

2. Apply adhesive spray to the back of the moon and apply it to the sky. Follow with the orange smoke. Note that the fabric for the yellow moon and the orange smoke may need to be doubled to prevent shadowing (page 15).

3. Carefully spray and apply Snoopy to the foreground.

4. Using a brush-out fabric marker, transfer detail lines for the bottom half of the moon, smoke lines throughout the orange, and wind lines in the purple sky.

5. With a narrow satin stitch, outline the upper edge of the orange smoke, starting at the edges of Snoopy's head and working out toward the outer edges. Then satin stitch the outlines of the moon—first the upper yellow half, then the lower orange half.

6. Outline Snoopy with a satin stitch. Use a narrow zigzag for the grassy foreground for a rougher appearance (Fig. 1).

7. Square up and trim the placemat to measure 9½" x 15½".

8. Following the table topper directions (pages 78–80), first apply a medium orange border to the placemat. Then apply a green and orange border with black cornerstones (Fig. 2).

9. Cut a 14" x 20" piece of backing. Layer with the quilt top and batting, and baste as needed. Quilt around Snoopy and the black foreground, the moon, the orange fog, and within the borders as shown. Then, using a brush-out fabric marker, trace movement lines within the orange fog and the wind swirls within the purple sky, and quilt. (See figure 3 and the quilt drawing on the CD for guidance.)

10. Cut 2 black strips 2¼" x WOF for the binding. Keeping the black and orange border at ¼" wide, apply the binding (page 24).

Fig. 1. Use a narrow zigzag for the grassy area.

Fig. 2. Green-orange borders with corner block

Fig. 3. Quilted smoke and wind lines

MERRY CHRISTMAS—Wallhanging

24½" x 35½", made by the author

Full-size patterns on the CD

Merry Christmas
Wallhanging

I used a variety of textured fabrics in this wallhanging, including pinwale corduroy for the Christmas tree, placed on the diagonal. The metallic tree lights are echoed in the metallic used for the silver stars and borders and the Christmas decorations are all satiny, reflective fabrics.

The shimmery fabrics work because they are different enough from the others to show off the ornaments, but not so different that they fight with everything else in the finished wallhanging

The snow is made from the wrong side of an off-white, flannel-backed coat lining. The shadows on the snow are of very fine blue netting, twisted and bunched to make the shadow under the tree darker than the rest. The background sky is the only print in this piece, and even then it is more of a gradation than a true print. It has a subtle spattering of shimmery gold highlights, reflecting the metallic used throughout the wallhanging

FABRICS AND SUPPLIES

Yardage

- ⅔ yard dark blue ombre gradation for the background
- 1 yard dark blue solid for the borders
- 1¼ yard silver metallic for the borders and binding
- ¼ yard dark blue or dark purple tulle, bridal illusion, or netting for the shadows
- ⅓ yard off-white napped fabric for snow
- ¼ yard white and silver print OR solid white for the lettering background

- ¾ yard muslin for ornaments, tree lights, and lettered semicircle
- 1¼ yards backing
- 29" x 40" batting

Scraps

You'll need squares approximately 5"x 5"

- Tan, textured fabric for Charlie Brown's hat
- Solid brown cotton for Charlie Brown's shoes and the tree trunk
- Brown leatherette for Charlie Brown's hat
- Dark red napped fabric for Charlie Brown's coat
- Blue denim for Charlie Brown's pants
- Bright red thin fleece for the stripes on Snoopy's hat
- White thin fleece for the stripes on Snoopy's hat
- Green napped fabric for Snoopy's and Woodstock's scarves and Woodstock's earmuffs
- Bright yellow thin fleece for Woodstock's body
- Heavy white cotton for Lucy's shoes
- Black leatherette for Lucy's shoes
- Gold metallic for the Christmas tree star
- Silver metallic for the stars in the sky
- Satins and/or metallics for the Christmas tree lights—light blue, red, orange, gold, dark blue, and aqua
- Bright cotton solids for Christmas tree decorations—red, light green, yellow, bright blue, and orange

Additional Scraps

- 10" x 10" white felt for the Christmas tree popcorn string
- 10" x 10" square dark lavender napped fabric (thin fleece or felt) for Lucy's hat, coat, and socks
- 10" x 10" square black cotton for Lucy's hair and Snoopy's ear and nose
- 6" x 6" square of white opaque fabric for Snoopy
- 10" x 10" square medium green pinwale corduroy for the Christmas tree
- 12" x 12" square of pink for the skin

Additional Supplies

- Machine embroidery thread—navy, silver, and lavender
- Black hand-embroidery thread
- 3 small black round beads for Lucy's coat
- ½" pompoms—1 each of white and purple
- Approximately 6 feet of thin, flexible tubing (Several types are available in home improvement stores; refrigerator tubing is one possibility.)
- Disappearing marker
- 4 – 9" x 12" sheets of Lite Steam-A-Seam 2
- 8 – 9" x 12" sheets of tracing paper
- 1 – 12" x 12" piece of transfer paper
- 4 – 12" x 12" pieces of wash-away stabilizer
- 7 – 9" x 12" sheets of tear-away stabilizer
- White marking pencil

CUTTING AND ASSEMBLING THE APPLIQUÉ

All cutting for the appliquéd area is done using the pattern pieces on the CD following the instructions in chapter 2. Assemble one appliqué element at a time—Snoopy, Woodstock, Charlie Brown, Lucy, and the Christmas tree. All patterns for appliqué pieces are already reversed; larger, background pieces are not reversed. Snoopy, Lucy, and Charlie Brown's eyes are free-motion machine embroidered; Woodstock's eye is satin stitched.

Charlie Brown

Note: The leatherette hat trim might melt when fused. Accordingly, the hat trim pieces are attached to the background with fabric adhesive spray, or a glue stick can also be used. The leatherette hat trim pieces are NOT reversed on the pattern sheets.

1. Create Charlie Brown's head. Double the skin fabric (page 15) if shadowing occurs.

2. Trace the pattern pieces for Charlie Brown's hat, jacket, pants, and shoes on the "not easy" liner of the fusible web. Remove the "easy" liner, and adhere each piece of fusible web to the wrong side of the appropriate fabric. Cut out the appliqué pieces and transfer any remaining embroidery details.

3. Layer all of Charlie Brown's pieces using the pressing sheet. Fuse all the pieces and allow to cool. Carefully remove them from the pressing sheet. Using adhesive spray or a glue stick, adhere the back corner of the hat and the back portion of the hat brim to the tan hat fabric. Later, you will attach the front edge of the brim directly to the background of the quilt with a glue stick. Note that the leatherette tassel is hanging free, and will be tucked under the top edge of the hat before the piece is adhered to the background.

Snoopy

1. Create Snoopy's head and body. Trace the pattern pieces on the "not easy" liner of the fusible web. Remove the "easy" liner and adhere each piece of fusible web to the wrong side of the appropriate fabric. Cut out the appliqué pieces. Apply fusible only to the part of the green scarf covering Snoopy's neck. The end of the scarf will hang free.

2. To create Snoopy's free-hanging ear, trace and cut out the ear pattern. Place this pattern on the wrong side of a small piece of black fabric and, using a white chalk pencil, trace around the pattern. Place another piece of black fabric under the first, right sides together. Pin together and sew the on the chalk line with a shortened stitch length. Leave the top edge open. Carefully clip all around the curved edge, turn, and press. Baste the ear closed on the top edge.

3. Transfer the embroidery details for Snoopy's face and body.

4. Set aside all pieces for Snoopy's hat and ear. Layer the remaining pieces using the pressing sheet, placing it over the quilt drawing on the CD for accuracy. Press, allow to cool, and remove from the pressing sheet. Set aside.

5. Layer Snoopy's red and white hat, placing the white pieces under the red. Fuse the hat pieces together, press, and allow to cool. Place Snoopy's body and head back on the pressing sheet, aligning the body and head with the pattern sheet. Layer the hat on Snoopy's head, covering the top of the head; fuse only the front portion of the hat in place to Snoopy's head. Do not fuse the back end of the hat to Snoopy's head. It must remain loose so it can be lifted to fit Snoopy's ear underneath.

Woodstock

1. Trace the pattern pieces for Woodstock, the earmuff, and the portion of the scarf which wraps around his neck onto the "not easy" liner on the fusible web. Remove the "easy" liner and adhere to the wrong side of the appropriate fabric. Cut out the appliqué pieces, and transfer any remaining embroidery details.

2. Layer Woodstock, his earmuff, and the neckband of the scarf on the pressing sheet, placing it over the pattern drawing for accuracy. Note that the tail of the scarf hangs free, and will be caught in satin stitching when embroidering Woodstock to the background. Fuse all pieces and allow to cool.

3. Transfer the embroidery details.

Lucy

1. Create Lucy's head. Double the skin fabric if shadowing occurs.

2. Trace the pattern pieces for Lucy's shoes, socks, legs, coat, hat, and hair on the "not easy" liner of the fusible web. Remove the "easy" liner and adhere each piece of fusible web to the wrong side of the appropriate fabric. Cut out the appliqué pieces, and transfer any remaining embroidery details.

3. Layer all of Lucy's pieces using the pressing sheet, placing it over the pattern drawing for accuracy. Fuse all the pieces and allow to cool. Carefully remove them from the pressing sheet.

4. Transfer the embroidery details.

Christmas Tree

1. Trace the pattern pieces for the tree and tree trunk on the "not easy" liner of the fusible web. For the Christmas tree, remove the "easy" liner and adhere the tree to the wrong side of the green corduroy so that the wales run diagonally across the tree. Adhere the tree trunk to the brown fabric. Cut out the appliqués.

2. For the Christmas tree bulbs hidden behind the tree, trace 3 pattern pieces on the "not easy" liner of the fusible web. Remove the "easy" liner and adhere the bulb shapes to the wrong sides of the aqua, gold, and dark blue metallic fabrics. Cut out the 3 bulbs.

3. For the ornament balls, trace the ornament pattern 7 times on the "not easy" liner of the fusible web. Remove the "easy" liner, and adhere the ornament shapes to the wrong sides of the appropriate fabrics—3 reds, 1 light green, 1 yellow, 1 bright blue, and 1 orange.

4. On the pressing sheet, and using the quilt drawing on the CD as a guide, layer the tree, the 3 partially hidden bulbs, the ornaments, and the tree trunk. Taking care with high temperatures on the metallic fabrics, fuse all the pieces, and allow to cool.

5. Create the three-dimensional tree star and 6 free-hanging light bulbs as follows:

   a. Bulbs are made of light blue (2), red (1), orange (2), and gold (1). The star is made of gold.

   b. Create a sandwich for each bulb (2 light blue, 1 red, 2 orange, and 1 gold) and 1 star (of gold), by layering 2 pieces of metallic fabric right-side out with a layer of muslin between. Pin together.

   c. On each sandwich, trace around patterns for the bulbs or star. With a shortened stitch length, stitch around each outline. Coat stitches lightly with seam sealant. Carefully cut out each shape just outside of the stitching line.

   d. Layer and pin all the shapes between 4 layers of water-soluble stabilizer (2 on top, 2 on the bottom). Press lightly. Carefully satin stitch around each shape. Soak the shapes in water for a few minutes to dissolve the stabilizer. Allow it to dry and press flat.

   e. Set aside.

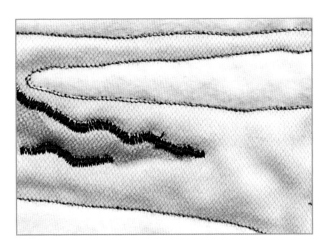

BACKGROUND AND SATIN STITCHING

1. Cut a sky 15" x 20" from blue ombré fabric. Using the pattern piece, cut snow from the right side of white flocked fabric. With fabric adhesive spray, adhere the snow to the sky using the quilt drawing on the CD as a placement guide. Using lavender thread and a wide satin stitch, stitch the edge of the snow in place. With a disappearing marker, mark lines for shadows on the snow fabric. Place a small piece of blue netting over each shadow area. Stitch over the shadow lines with a slight zigzag stitch. Cut the netting away close to the stitching lines and carefully apply seam sealant to the cut edges (Fig. 1).

Fig. 1. Cut netting close to the stitching line and treat with seam sealant.

2. Using the quilt drawing on the CD as a guide, place appliqués on the background, with Charlie Brown behind Snoopy and Woodstock to the left of the tree, and Lucy to the right of the tree.

3. Press and fuse the appliqués to the background as follows:

    a. In areas that lie on top of the snow shadows, take care not to touch the netting with the iron. Either use a mini-iron or, instead of ironing, use a glue stick to attach these areas.

    b. For Charlie Brown, tuck the hat tassel into the top of the hat before fusing it to the background.

    c. For Snoopy, tuck the ear under the edge of the hat and the hanging portion of the scarf under the neckband before fusing to the background.

    d. For Woodstock, tuck the hanging portion of his scarf under the neckband before fusing it to the background. After completing the satin stitching, cut a small strip of the earmuff fabric, ⅛" x ¼". Place it on Woodstock's head, between the earmuff and up and through the head feathers. Tack or glue in place.

4. Satin stitch the characters to the background working from the middle toward the outer edges.

5. Satin stitch the tree to the background. Tack the metallic bulbs to the tree at the top of each bulb so that they hang downward. Tack a strand of black embroidery thread along the top edge of the bulbs (Fig. 2).

6. With disappearing marker, trace 12 popcorn shapes onto white felt. Cut the pieces out and string them through the centers onto a piece of black embroidery thread, spacing the popcorn centers approximately 1"–1½" apart. Tie a knot in the thread right before and after each piece of popcorn to hold it in place. Tack the popcorn strands in place on the tree (Fig. 3), following the quilt drawing on the CD.

7. Tack the gold star to the top of the tree. Finish the base of the tree by folding and twisting a small piece of blue netting (measuring approximately ½" x 6") so that it forms thin layers. Catch the netting in the satin stitching under the tree, first along the upper ground line and then again underneath to complete the shadows. Clip away the excess netting and carefully apply seam sealant to the edges (Fig. 4).

Fig. 2. Tack light bulbs to the Christmas tree.

8. Follow the quilt drawing on the CD and fuse the 5 silver stars to sky. Stitch with a narrow zigzag stitch using silver thread. Tack the pompoms in place on Lucy's and Snoopy's hats and tack down a small bow made of black embroidery floss onto each of Lucy's shoes (Fig. 5). Sew 3 small black beads to the front edge of Lucy's coat.

FINISHING

1. Square up and trim the panel to measure 19" wide x 20½" tall. Crosscut 4 strips 1" x the width of fabric (WOF) of silver metallic fabric. Add to the sides, then to the top and bottom of the panel (page 23).

2. Crosscut 3 strips 3" x WOF of solid blue fabrics. Apply first to the sides, then the bottom edge of the panel. Using the large-size semicircle pattern on the CD, cut a semicircle from solid blue fabric. With right sides together, and adjusting the long edge of the semicircle to fit the quilt, sew the blue semicircle to the top edge. (**Note:** The blue semicircle is sewn directly to the edge of the upper silver border.)

3. Using the medium-size semicircle pattern on the CD, cut 1 semicircle from silver metallic fabric and 1 from muslin. Place right sides together and sew, using a ½" seam allowance. Carefully clip the curved edge of the seam allowance. Cut a small slit in the center of the muslin (taking care not to clip the metallic fabric) and turn. Press carefully from the muslin side to avoid touching the silver fabric with the iron.

Fig. 3. Tack the popcorn strand to the Christmas tree.

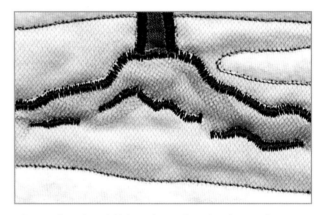

Fig. 4. Catch additional netting in the satin stitching at the bottom of the tree. Clip away the excess.

Fig. 5. Use embroidery floss laces for Lucy's shoes.

4. Using the small-size semicircle pattern on the CD, cut 1 semicircle from white/silver Christmas print and 1 from muslin. Transfer the "Merry Christmas" wording to the right side of the print semicircle, centering it as indicated. Stabilizing the fabric as necessary, satin stitch the wording in silver embroidery thread, then outline around the letters with dark blue embroidery thread (Fig. 6). Using a ½" seam allowance, sew the 2 semicircles right sides together. Carefully clip the curved edge of the seam allowance. Cut a small slit in the center of the muslin (taking care not to clip the print fabric), and turn. Press carefully.

5. Center the lettered semicircle on top of the silver semicircle. Pin carefully and sew in place with a narrow blind hemstitch or invisibly hand stitch in place.

6. Place the lettered/silver semicircle on the blue background, maintaining 2" blue borders. Pin carefully and sew in place with a narrow blind hemstitch or invisibly hand stitch.

7. Press the quilt top from the back. Cut a piece of backing 29" x 40". Layer it with batting and the quilt top. Baste as needed. Quilt around the characters and main elements. Then, using brush-out fabric marker, trace wind lines onto the background sky. See the pattern drawing on the CD for guidance. Quilt over the lines.

8. Carefully trim the batting and backing even with the top of the quilt. Bind with 126" (3½ yards) of 3½" wide silver metallic strips cut on the bias (page 24).

9. Apply a premade sleeve to the back of the wallhanging. Measure around the top curved edge of the quilt with a tape measure. Cut the sleeve to that measurement plus 1". Turn the ends of the sleeve to the inside and stitch. Machine gather the bottom edge of the sleeve with a long machine stitch, ¼" in from the edge. Stitch a second row of gathering within the ¼" allowance. Pull up the 2 rows of gathering until the sleeve fits within the curved area of the quilt back. Pin and hand stitch in place along both long edges, leaving 2" open at the very top edge (Fig. 7).

10. Cut a strip of dark blue fabric 4" x 7". Pin the long edges right sides together and stitch. Turn and press flat. Bring the short, raw edges together and insert them into the 2" opening in the seam of the top of the hanging sleeve. Stitch the opening closed, catching in the raw edges of the tab and leaving the top of the tab free for hanging.

11. Using thin flexible tubing, cut 1 or 2 lengths equal to the length of the sleeve. Insert the tubing into the sleeve to hold the quilt flat (Fig. 8).

12. Tack the ends of the sleeve closed to keep the tubes from slipping out (Fig. 9).

Fig. 6. Center the wording on the semicircle.

Fig. 7. Gather and hand stitch the sleeve to the curve.

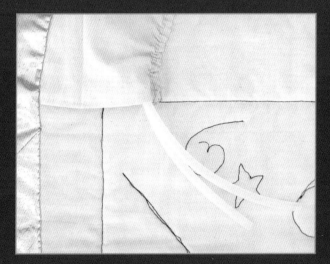

Fig. 8. Insert one or two lengths of tubing into the sleeve.

Fig. 9. Tack the ends of the sleeve closed.

PHOTOS ON THIS PAGE BY KATHLEEN SHEA

FINAL THOUGHTS

For those who would like to learn more about Charles Schulz and the wonderful legacy he left to the world, please take a trip to Santa Rosa, California, and visit the Charles M. Schulz Museum (www.schulzmuseum.org). The museum houses the largest collection of Peanuts strips in the world, has a research center, and displays a myriad of permanent and changing exhibits. Be sure not to miss the museum gift shop!

While you're visiting the museum, take some time to also visit Snoopy's Home Ice, The Redwood Empire Ice Arena (www.snoopyhomeice.com), and Snoopy's Gallery and Gift Shop (www.snoopygift.com). All are located within walking distance of each other and the visit makes for a lovely day!

There have been countless Peanuts books, books written about Peanuts, and about Charles M. Schulz. I recommend these:

Bang, Derrick, *50 Years of Happiness: A Tribute to Charles M. Schulz* (Santa Rosa, California: Charles M. Schulz Museum, 1999). ISBN 0-9685574-0-6

Johnson, Rheta Grimsley, *Good Grief: The Story of Charles M. Schulz* (New York: Pharos Books, 1989). ISBN 0-88687-553-6

Kidd, Chip (ed.), *Peanuts: The Art of Charles M. Schulz* (New York: Pantheon Books, 2001). ISBN 0-375-42097-5

Larkin, David (ed.), *Peanuts: A Golden Celebration: The Art and the Story of the World's Best-Loved Comic Strip* (New York: HarperCollins, 1999).

There are a huge number of online resources available to help you learn about Peanuts. Two of note are:

www.peanutscollectorclub.com—the website of Peanuts Collector Club (the "official" club for Peanuts collectors)

Be sure to visit the Peanuts Collector Club page on www.facebook.com.

www.fivecentsplease.com—a website with more information about Peanuts than you ever thought existed!

Finally, the publishing company Fantagraphics (www.fantagraphics.com) is currently publishing the Peanuts strips *in their entirety*, from 1950 to the end, in a series of ongoing books. These books make up a truly attractive set of reading material for any Peanuts fan!

ABOUT THE AUTHOR

Kathleen Shea's journey into quilting the Peanuts characters began when, at an early age, her mother (patiently!) taught her to sew. An enthusiastic learner, Kathleen was sewing on her own by the age of eight. At the same time, she was also discovering the wonder of the Peanuts characters! During the time she was growing up in the 1960s, Charles Schulz's Peanuts gang was becoming a part of everyone's world, and Snoopy was quickly becoming Kathleen's best friend!

So, while continuing to perfect her sewing skills, Kathleen also started collecting—Peanuts dolls, banks, banners, books—anything and everything that depicted Snoopy, Charlie Brown, and all their friends. She continued sewing (first making her own clothes, and later concentrating on quilts and appliqué), and kept up with the Peanuts gang by reading the phenomenally popular comic strip in the newspaper every day.

In 1984, Kathleen graduated with a bachelor of fine arts degree in design from the Fashion Institute of Technology and later obtained a law degree from St. John's University. She has authored several articles in journals and periodicals. As a contributing member of the Peanuts Collector's Club, she also wrote a quarterly column for the club's newsletter for several years.

It was through her involvement with the Peanuts Collector's Club that Kathleen first learned of the wonderful organization, Canine Companions for Independence (CCI). CCI has been the designated charity of the Peanuts Collector's Club since the Club's founder, Andrea Podley, selected it as such years ago. CCI is a non-profit organization that—free of charge—provides highly-trained assistance dogs to people with disabilities. Located in Santa Rosa, CA, CCI is recognized worldwide for the excellence of both its dogs, and its overall program. Kathleen is happy to donate 10% of her proceeds from this book to CCI!

Peanuts®– Quilted Celebrations is Kathleen's first book. It is most certainly an inevitable outgrowth of her love of sewing and her obsession with Peanuts! Alongside the growing popularity of quilting (this craft has mushroomed in the United States in recent years), the Peanuts gang has truly become a force of pop culture all over the world. Though Charles Schulz succumbed to cancer in the year 2000 (passing away the night before his last strip was published), the popularity of the characters he created continues to grow.

Kathleen is thrilled to bring the Peanuts gang—in fabric and thread—to quilters and hopes her patterns inspire Peanuts collectors to try their hands at quilting, too!

OTHER AQS BOOKS

This is only a small selection of the books available from the American Quilter's Society. AQS books are known worldwide for timely topics, clear writing, beautiful color photos, and accurate illustrations and patterns. The following books are available from your local bookseller, quilt shop, or public library.

#1548. . . . . $21.95

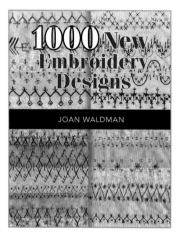

#1644. . . . . $24.95

#8764. . . . . $22.95

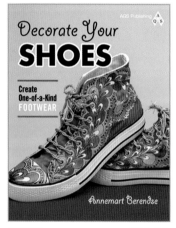

#8766. . . . . $19.95

#8347. . . . . $24.95

#8664. . . . . $19.95

#1590. . . . . $12.95

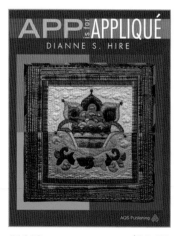

#1419. . . . . $24.95

#1248. . . . . $24.95

LOOK for these books nationally.
CALL or **VISIT** our website at

1-800-626-5420
www.AmericanQuilter.com